FRENCH CHÂTEAU LIVING

THE CHÂTEAU DU LUDE

FRENCH CHÂTEAU LIVING

THE CHÂTEAU DU LUDE

Text **Barbara de Nicolaÿ** and **Christine Toulier**
With the assistance of **Christiane de Nicolaÿ-Mazery**
Photography **Eric Sander**

Flammarion

Contents

Foreword 8
Introduction 11

I

THE CHÂTEAU DU LUDE: A THOUSAND YEARS OF HISTORY 23

The Fortress of Anjou (Thirteenth–Fifteenth Centuries) 24

The Angel of Le Lude 32

The Château under the de Daillon Family,
from Earldom to Dukedom (1457–1685) 40

Duvelaër of the East India Company
and his Descendants (1750–1810) 62

The Talhouët-Roy Family at Le Lude:
New Vistas for the Château (1810–1948) 118

The Nicolaÿ Family at Le Lude
(1948 to the present day) 150

II

LIFE AT LE LUDE 169

III

THE GARDENS: A RENAISSANCE 231

The Gardens at Le Lude 234

The Prix Pierre-Joseph Redouté:
A Tribute to Books about Gardens 252

Bibliography 260
Acknowledgments 261

PAGE 2
The south wing of the château, in iconic Renaissance style, looks out
over the terraced gardens. A balcony supported by two columns communicates
between the *appartamento nobile* and the large dining room.

PAGES 4–5
Attributed to Paul Lafargue, *West Elevation
of the Château du Lude*, c.1911, ink and wash.

FACING PAGE
Detail of a candelabrum pilaster in the north vestibule.

Foreword

As I travel around the châteaux and castles of France filming my television series *Secrets d'Histoire* or *Le Village préféré des Français*, I am struck by a curious paradox that never ceases to surprise me. French people adore their heritage and their history, and they are always prepared to go out of their way to visit an ancestral home. At the same time, though, they view these ancient buildings—however mistakenly—as the outward signs of great wealth, and as powerful symbols of the privileges that were abolished by the Revolution. What are these privileges, exactly? The undeniable privilege of living in such historic surroundings, certainly, steeped in beauty as they are, filled with lovely furniture and works of art, and surrounded by gardens and parks of timeless splendor. But these exceptional buildings are a great responsibility, too, and as we marvel at their outward magnificence we often give little thought to all the work and sacrifice that go into their upkeep. And yet, the families who have inherited the stewardship of these jewels of French history and architecture shoulder this burden cheerfully, without a thought for how much simpler—if more painful—it might be to give all this up, in exchange for a comfortable, centrally-heated apartment by the seaside.

The magic of what the French confusingly call *la vie de château*—shorthand for a life of luxury and indulgence—lies in this ambivalence. Châteaux and fortresses fire our fantasies and our imagination, but most of the visitors who marvel at their ancient walls, lofty halls, historic art collections, and immaculately tended gardens could scarcely imagine living inside their walls: they may be filled with fascination, wonder, and astonishment, but only rarely will they be filled with envy. At the same time, one of the more intangible but nonetheless seductive charms of these ancient buildings lies in that inimitably French art de vivre that they hand down from one generation to the next, and in the perpetuation of an historic heritage that the French State on its own would struggle to preserve, were it not for those who live in them. The Château du Lude belongs to this magic circle of ancestral houses that have retained their soul, and that remain a family home. The Nicolaÿ family are staunch defenders of this heritage, and of the necessity of protecting it for future generations. I recall my first visit to Le Lude, in the company of the late Comtesse de Paris, who was delighted to see her cousin, Princess Pia Maria d'Orléans-Bragance, a great and courageous spirit who, following the premature death of her husband, the Comte de Nicolaÿ, after just six years of marriage, was determined to preserve Le Lude while also raising her two sons. Thus it was—necessity being the mother of invention—that the first "son et lumière" (sound and light) performance in France was created. Against all the odds, Le Lude has remained a family home, open to the public and offering a warm welcome.

The most northerly of all the châteaux of the Loire, Le Lude is an historic monument that has witnessed six centuries of building and alterations. More than this, it has an atmosphere and a spirit that owe everything to the family who have made it their home for over two hundred and fifty years. Each succeeding generation has striven to make its own additions, literally or symbolically, making the house and grounds increasingly accessible to growing numbers of visitors, and bringing the glorious gardens alive—most notably through the Fête des Jardiniers, now an annual fixture in the gardening calendar, when the prestigious Prix Pierre-Joseph Redouté is awarded. The magic spell with which the Château du Lude now enchants its visitors is testament to Comte Louis-Jean de Nicolaÿ and his wife Barbara, and to their faithful stewardship of this ancient building. They are determined to ensure that it retains all its charms as a family home while also welcoming the public. In so doing, they also continue to pay tribute to those qualities of elegance, savoir-vivre, and refinement that are so inimitably, and I hope eternally, French.

Stéphane Bern

FACING PAGE
The southwest tower. The west-facing dormer window, with its slender mullions,
cuts across the chemin de ronde and is surmounted by an earl's coronet.
Underneath it is a pair of medallions carved with two facing heads, male and female,
which may be portraits of Jehan III de Daillon, first Comte du Lude, and his wife.

Introduction

*R*uins of ancient fortresses, built by feudal lords to defend their lands, are dotted all across the French countryside, and none more so than in the valley of the River Loir. But at the Château du Lude time did not stop in the medieval period. Five centuries of history have shaped this château, developing it from a medieval stronghold into a Renaissance palace reflecting the power of its seneschals and the glory of France. Today, this magnificent residence, with its graceful crenellated turrets, has many surprises in store for its visitors.

In the beginning was Anjou

Set in the marches of Anjou in the valley of the Loir, close to the regions of Maine and Touraine, Le Lude has occupied this strategic site since the ninth century. Its name derives from the Roman fortifications that stood here, *castellum lusdii*, which in turn took their name from the river *Ledus* or *Ledum*. The fortified settlement of Le Lude was surrounded by rudimentary ramparts, and was repeatedly attacked by the Normans, whose incursions into the region followed the courses of the River Loire and the River Maine. Gradually, with building work stretching from the thirteenth to the fifteenth century, the settlement gained a stone-built fortress. This stronghold was constructed on an impressive scale—it was big enough to accommodate a garrison of two thousand men—owing to its strategic position on the frontier of the kingdom of Anjou, in a region ravaged by the Hundred Years' War.

From the tenth to the fifteenth century, ownership of Le Lude lay continuously in the hands of great feudal lords. Initially, it was the property of the Counts of Anjou, including the feared Foulques Nerra; Jean de Brienne, King of Jerusalem; and the lords of Beaumont and Vendôme. In the Middle Ages, the fortress bristled with every type of fortification: barbicans and great towers were constructed, the oldest of them resting on walls that were over twenty-six feet thick; a dry moat, both deep and wide, was excavated; and a masonry spur and ramparts were erected along the banks of the Loir. Visitors who climb down into the dry moat today can still gain a commanding and highly evocative view of these imposing fortifications.

All these measures were to prove effective, first when the castle was besieged by the Duke of Brittany, and in 1370, during the Hundred Years' War, at the bloody Battle of Pontvallain. Captain Guillaume de Méron successfully fended off two attacks by English forces under Sir Robert Knolles, who had occupied the town with ten thousand knights. Half a century later, however, in 1425, the castle fell to the Earl of Warwick, victorious from his conquest of the province of Maine. Two years later, Jacques de Beaumanoir, Ambroise de Loré, and Gilles de Rais, the notorious Bluebeard, battled the English again at the side of Joan of Arc. They managed to liberate the castle, now badly damaged, but at the cost of terrible bloodshed. With the development of the large guns known as bombards, the attackers were able to use gunpowder to inflict serious damage on the fortress walls and buildings. It would take many years for Le Lude to patch up its wounds, and meanwhile, with the peaceful reign of René I, known as "Good" King René, Anjou entered the Renaissance.

FACING PAGE
One of the windows in the south vestibule.

French Château Living: The Château du Lude

A new era was now beginning for Le Lude, closely linked with the rise to power of the de Daillon family from Poitou. Jehan de Daillon bought the castle and lands of Le Lude in 1457, and until 1685 it was to be handed down from father to son, over seven generations of the family. All of them occupied positions of major influence at court and in the army. Although not a royal castle, Le Lude was nonetheless close to the center of power. The spectacular transformation of the austere fortress into a glittering palace was the physical expression of the inexorable rise of a single family in the service of the French kings.

Yet matters did not get off to an auspicious start. Jehan de Daillon, at this point chamberlain to the Dauphin—the future Louis XI—picked the wrong side, supporting King Charles VII in his disputes with his son. After his accession to the throne, Louis XI persecuted de Daillon relentlessly, forcing him to hide away in a cave a few miles from Le Lude for the next seven years. Restored to royal favor in 1468, de Daillon succeeded in regaining the trust of the king, who made him chamberlain again before appointing him governor of Poitou, captain of the *cent lances des ordonnances du roi*, and general of the armies of Roussillon and Picardy. So skilled a negotiator was he that de Daillon became known as the "master of diplomacy."

His son, Jacques de Daillon, succeeded Jehan from 1481 to 1533. Valiant on the battlefield, Jacques distinguished himself fighting alongside François I during the Italian Wars, notably at the battles of Fontarabbia and Pavia. He married Madeleine d'Illiers, who worked closely with him on the projects he embarked upon to embellish the castle. As an indirect consequence of François I's spirit of conquest, the Angevin residence was remodeled in the Renaissance taste imported from Italy.

Jacques' son, Jean de Daillon, on whom François I conferred the title Comte du Lude, made Le Lude his residence from 1533 to 1557. Governor of Poitou, Seneschal of Anjou, and Lieutenant General of Guyenne, he married Anne de Bastarnay, who brought to the marriage the vast forests of Champchevrier, where he was able to indulge in the pleasures of the hunt. Jean built a second château, intending to welcome royal guests there.

Guy de Daillon (*c.*1530–1585), brought up at the royal court as page of honor to Henri de Navarre, inherited his father's titles. He married Jeanne de La Fayette, who played an essential part in the interior decorations of the château. The Studiolo, with its carefully preserved wall paintings dating from this period, could now be admired once more.

Next came François de Daillon (1570–1619), who was famed at court for his wit and bons mots. He had the privilege of welcoming two sovereigns to Le Lude on several occasions. It was at Le Lude that Henri IV, on his way to celebrate mass for Corpus Christi at Chartres in 1594, took part in his first Catholic procession after his conversion. Four years later, Henri stayed at Le Lude again after signing the Edict of Nantes, this time accompanied by Gabrielle d'Estrées, who had just given birth to their third child. Then in 1619, Louis XIII stopped there on his way to Touraine to meet his mother, Marie de' Medici, and later returned to take part in hunts held in his honor in the forests of Champchevrier.

Timoléon de Daillon (1600–1651), courtier and soldier, retired to Le Lude to complete his embellishments to the château and gardens, sparing no expense in his efforts to give this family domain the appearance of a minor royal court. Timoléon was succeeded on his death by his only son, Henri. Brought up at court, Henri rose to the highest of ranks, including Lieutenant General of the Army, Governor of Versailles, and Grand Master of the Artillery. In 1675, the Le Lude estates gained further prestige when Louis XIV raised them to the status of a

FACING PAGE
Portrait of Henri IV as a Roman Emperor in the north vestibule
decorated in the neoclassical style. Henri IV, newly converted to Catholicism,
brandishes a cross and holds a palm leaf, symbol of martyrdom.

PAGES 14–15
The view of the château from the southeast clearly shows the two major periods of building at Le Lude:
the sixteenth century, with its crenellations and stone mullions; and the eighteenth century, with its evenly
spaced bays with bosses, its symmetry and regularity highlighted by a central pediment.

French Château Living: The Château du Lude

duchy. His estates at Saint-Germain-en-Laye and his duties left Henri, now Duc de Daillon, little leisure time to spend on his lands at Le Lude, however, and they became merely a source of revenue for him. At the court of the Sun King, Henri's lively wit and sparkling repartee were famous. Henri married the strong-minded Eléonore de Bouillé, who was only happy when riding to hounds and was known as the "great huntress." His second wife was Marguerite de Béthune, daughter of the Duc de Sully and lady-in-waiting to the Duchesse de Bourgogne. The Duc du Lude died in 1685, without issue and crippled by debts, bequeathing Le Lude to his nephew, the Duc de Roquelaure. The château was subsequently inherited by the Ducs de Rohan, who, having no ancestral link with their Angevin estates, gradually abandoned them. In 1751, the Château du Lude—by now suffering the effects of the prolonged absences of its owners since the death of Henri, Duc de Daillon—was put up for sale.

It was at this point that the fortunes of the Château du Lude underwent a sea change, with the arrival of a nabob from the Orient. Joseph Julien Duvelaër came from a family of Dutch privateers who had settled in St Malo. The son of the director of the French East India Company and owner of his own merchant fleet, he ran the French trading post in Canton, where his business interests flourished. Having made his fortune, Duvelaër retired to France with his Chinese wife. There he bought from the Rohan heirs the château and estates of Le Lude, consisting of villages, farms, mills, tolls, and several thousand hectares of land, while Louis XV elevated him to the rank of Comte du Lude. When he died without issue, Duvelaër bequeathed his estate to his niece, the Marquise de La Vieuville.

The marquise rapidly fell under the spell of the château and decided to move there, leaving her husband behind in Brittany, where he was governor of the Parlement. The major campaign of refurbishment and modernization that she embarked upon was interrupted by the Revolution, during which she chose to remain at the château in order to ensure its protection during this time of upheaval. Her greatest champions during this period of successive incursions by Royalists and Revolutionaries were the inhabitants of Le Lude, who united around their chatelaine, as is borne out by correspondence from the period preserved at the château. Her husband was less fortunate, however: in 1792, at the age of eighty-four, he was sent to the guillotine in Rennes.

The marquise left the château to her daughter, who was married to Louis Céleste de Talhouët. For the next century and a half, this new family, which played a prominent part in public life, was to link its fortunes with the Château du Lude.

ABOVE
The frontispiece of the volume of maps of the estate drawn up by Édouard André
for the Marquis de Talhouët-Roy in 1880. The frieze of Virginia creeper that clothed the terrace
wall over a length of some two hundred yards can clearly be seen.

FACING PAGE
Portrait of Marguerite-Louise-Suzanne de Béthune, Comtesse de Guiche, second Duchesse du Lude,
by Louis-Ferdinand Elle, oil on canvas, preserved at the Château de Sully-sur-Loire (Loiret).

French Château Living: The Château du Lude

Louis Céleste de Talhouët, born in Brittany, became one of the first presidents of the Sarthe regional council, while his wife was lady-in-waiting to Empress Josephine and Empress Marie-Louise. Their son, Frédéric, gained the rank of colonel under the Empire, and fought under Napoleon at major battles from Iéna to Borodino. Seriously wounded during the retreat from Moscow, he owed his life to the devotion of his troops, who carried him to an "ambulance" of the Grande Armée. In 1814, he rallied in support of the Bourbons, pursuing his military career as a field marshal in the royal guard. On his retirement from the army, he made his home at the Château du Lude and entered politics, becoming president of the Sarthe regional council in his turn. Frédéric's wife, Alexandrine, was the eldest daughter of Comte Antoine Roy, tenderer of the last Duc de Bouillon. Roy, a lawyer and politician, whose life is like a novel, spent the Revolutionary period defending his property on all sides and on every front—including the National Convention, Napoleon, and Beauharnais—before being appointed Minister of Finance under Louis XVIII and Charles X, by whom he was ennobled. He demanded that Alexandrine retain the family name upon her marriage in 1817, as a large part of her inheritance was tied up in the Château du Lude. His younger daughter married Admiral de Rigny.

Frédéric and Alexandrine's son, Auguste, Marquis de Talhouët-Roy, succeeded his father as mayor of Le Lude, regional councillor, parliamentary deputy, senator, and Minister of Public Works under Napoleon III. He opposed the coup d'état of Louis Napoleon Bonaparte in 1851, and was briefly imprisoned at Vincennes, before serving as Minister of Public Works under the Second Empire in 1870. He and his wife, Léonie Honnorez, a wealthy Belgian heiress, embarked on major refurbishments of the Château du Lude.

They were succeeded by their son, René de Talhouët-Roy, both in regional politics and in the running of the Le Lude estate. Like many of his predecessors, René, who was mayor of Le Lude for fifty-six years, preferred his estates in the Sarthe to life in Paris. In the twentieth century, the château offered shelter to his family throughout both world wars. In 1927, the marquis, whose estates covered six thousand hectares, had the château officially classified as an historic monument. A dedicated huntsman, he founded the Talhouët deer hunt.

On the death of the marquis in 1948, the château passed to his grandson, Comte René de Nicolaÿ. Following the latter's untimely death six years later, his widow, née Princess Pia d'Orléans-Bragance, took over the management of the estate. She breathed new life into Le Lude with the creation of a "son et lumière" (sound and light show). The first of its kind, this spectacular show related the history of the château, with a cast of three hundred and fifty, all drawn from the local population. It attracted nearly five million spectators in almost forty years.

Today, the château is home to her son, Comte Louis-Jean de Nicolaÿ, Senator for the Sarthe region and Mayor of Le Lude. Since our marriage in 1980, four children and two grandchildren have arrived to complete the picture. Together we have worked to restore and develop the gardens, following in the spirit of openness, hospitality, and conservation that has always guided family tradition at Le Lude.

PAGES 18–19
A filmy early morning mist over the Loir, beneath the Jardin de la Source.
FACING PAGE
The Chinese pavilion was the principal garden ornament designed
by the landscape architect Édouard André for the Jardin de la Source.
The pavilion concealed a hydraulic ram that until recently
pumped up river water to irrigate the gardens.

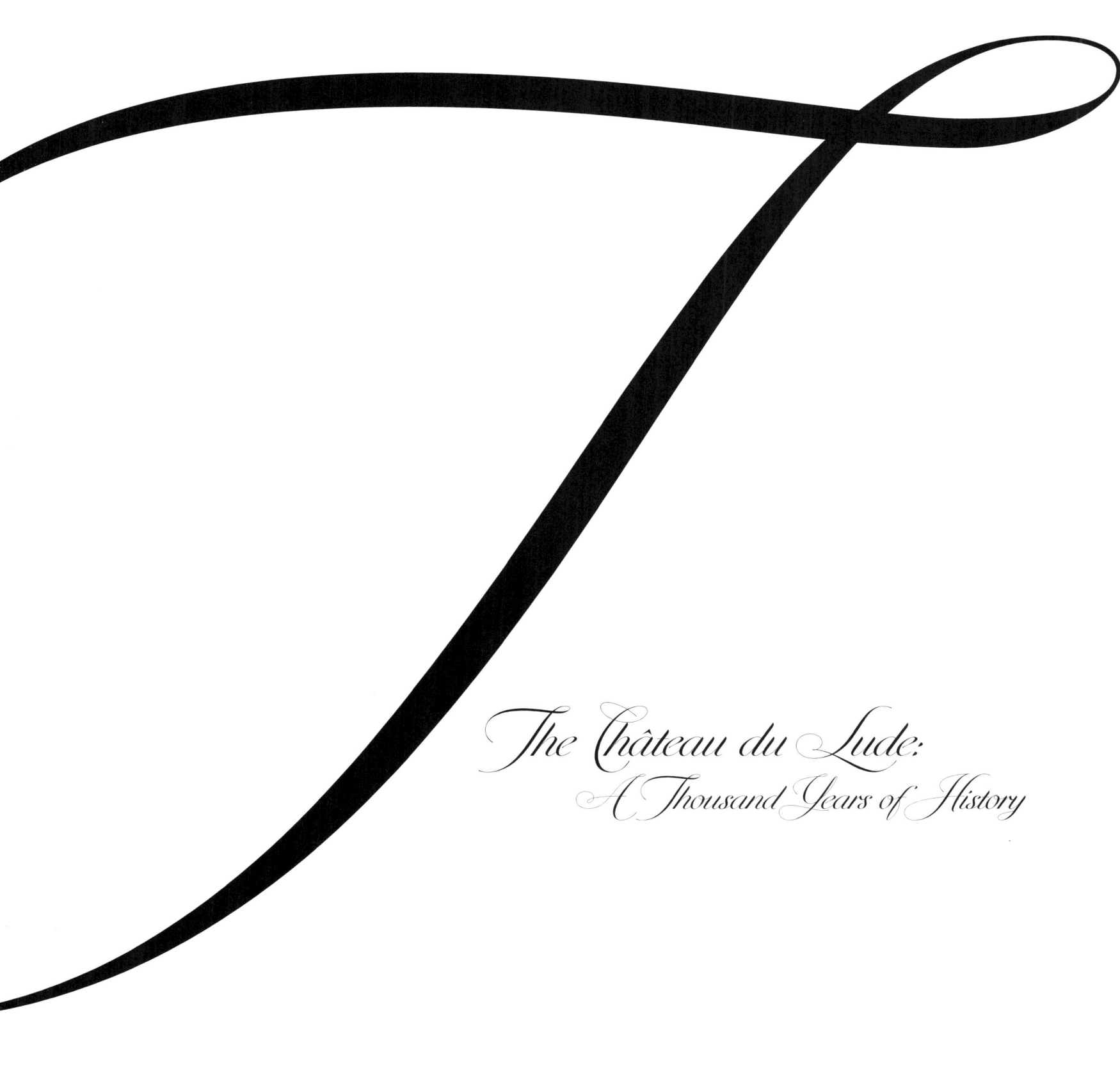

The Château du Lude:
A Thousand Years of History

French Château Living: The Château du Lude

The Fortress of Anjou
Thirteenth–Fifteenth Centuries

One of the earliest contemporary references to a fortress at Le Lude comes in a charter relating to military incursions by the Normans, the formidable invaders from the north who mounted daring assaults along the course of the Loire and Maine rivers.

The original fortress, on top of which the present château now stands, was built from the thirteenth century, at a time when developments in the art of warfare made it necessary to construct more solid defenses.

A few hundred years later, a new threat arose from the dynastic struggle between the Plantagenets and the Valois. France and England were locked into the long, drawn-out conflict of the Hundred Years' War, which threw the whole region into a state of turmoil. The Battle of Pontvallain, at which Bertrand du Guesclin won a decisive French victory, was fought barely a dozen or so miles from Le Lude, and bore witness to the merciless ferocity of contemporary warfare. The fortress was besieged on several occasions, while the periods of truce in the intervening periods were used to strengthen its fortifications by adding barbicans, defensive walls, plunging ditches, monumental towers, drawbridges, and defensive spurs. Ultimately, the fortress boasted the full panoply of defensive works, emerging as a consummate example of the military genius of the Middle Ages.

All these dramatic features may still be seen today, and are especially evocative when viewed from the bottom of the dry moat. The cellars and underground passages are carved out of the soft, white tuffeau limestone that is such a ubiquitous feature of the Loire Valley, and the rubble extracted was used on site to reinforce the structure of the corridors and armories. The quarries formed endless underground galleries that still lie beneath the streets of the town.

The impression of monumental impregnability was underscored by the methods of construction used. The walls, built according to the Roman technique, consisted of two external walls of dressed stone infilled with masonry rubble, and ranged in thickness from twelve feet to as many as thirty. The difficulties that had to be surmounted in the Renaissance, when these walls had to be pierced to create windows, may well be imagined.

The period after the Hundred Years' War, in the mid-fifteenth century, was one of desolation for Le Lude and for Anjou in general. Prosperity was only to return in the Renaissance, under "Good" King René, who ushered in a flourishing period in both the economy and the arts, untroubled by war. Many building projects were embarked upon throughout the region, the nobility began to reinvest money in their abandoned and neglected castles, and Jehan de Daillon from Poitou, chamberlain to Louis XI, became the new lord of Le Lude.

PAGE 22
View from the grand terrace of the farmlands on the right bank of the Loir.
FACING PAGE
In spring, a profusion of flowering shrubs smothers
the wall under the long terrace, with syringas, spiraeas, and deutzias
alternating between buttresses of clipped yew.

"The Château du Lude is a historic monument, its origins lost in the obscurity of the feudal age. As early as the tenth century, a baronial fortress stood here, to defend the marches of Anjou on the border with the province of Maine."

Le Monde illustré, no. 28, October 24, 1857

FACING PAGE
Plan of Le Lude around 1770, by Boullard, architect of Château-du-Loir. The château of the last of the de Daillons still turned its back on the town.

The Château du Lude: A Thousand Years of History

"This treasure of the Renaissance, on which modern science now shines its light, did not spring fully formed from the overweening dreams of a feudal lord bent on flaunting his power. It stands as the reminder of a thousand years of endeavor, to build it, to embellish it and to defend it."

Les Glorieuses et Fastueuses Soirées au bord du Loir,
complete performance script by **MICHEL MISSOFFE**

FACING PAGE
This narrow, winding staircase with a balustrade in tuffeau stone leads down to the cellars beneath the northwest tower of the north wing.

PAGES 30–31
The ancient drawbridge was demolished in the late eighteenth century and replaced with a fixed bridge spanning the dry moat on the south side of the château.

French Château Living: The Château du Lude

The Angel of Le Lude

"LE XXVIIᵉ JOUR DE MARS / L'AN MIL CCCC LX + XV JEHAN BARBET DIT DE LION FIST CEST ANGELOT"

*On the 27th day of March in the year 1460 + 15
Jean Barbet, called of Lyon, made this angel*

In the great hall of the château there stands a bronze statue of an angel, a figure of striking beauty with a remarkable history. It has been said that this bronze-cast masterpiece of fifteenth-century Gothic art could almost be a figure by Memling or Van Eyck. The exquisite delicacy of the figure's features and the harmonious folds of his robe are undiminished by the patina of the bronze. The body is cast in a single piece, with the finely worked wings attached by means of pins. The facial features are set in an expression of serene and quiet dignity. The angel holds a cross in his left hand, while with the index finger of his right hand he makes an enigmatic gesture.

Because of its beauty and rarity, this work has been the object of a considerable amount of research, which means that we can now trace some of the mysterious steps of its journey to the present day. One thing is certain: this angel, made by the bronze-founder Jean (Jehan) Barbet in 1475 and bearing his signature, is the only French fifteenth-century monumental bronze to have survived into modern times. It was probably made to decorate one of the spires or the altar of the Sainte-Chapelle in Paris. At the Revolution, it is believed to have been sold off as property of the State. But how did it come to be at Le Lude?

Around 1820, a friendship grew up between General Frédéric de Talhouët and Alexandre du Sommerard, founder of the Musée de Cluny. It was this friendship that lay behind the latter's decision to cede this important piece from his collection to the château in the Sarthe. The general's son, Auguste de Talhouët-Roy, moved by the angel's beauty, installed it in a place of honor at the foot of the grand staircase of the château's new tower. In this prominent spot it attracted all eyes, greeting visitors as they crossed the threshold.

FACING PAGE AND PAGES 34–37
The Angel of Le Lude is the only French fifteenth-century bronze monumental
statue known to have survived to the present day. The reverse side of one
of the angel's wings is inscribed with the signature of its maker, an extremely
rare detail in a work of this period.

The Château du Lude: A Thousand Years of History

The bronze angel seemed to have found permanent refuge at Le Lude. In the next generation, however, the art dealer Jacques Seligmann managed to persuade the Marquis de Talhouët-Roy to sell the angel, and it was taken back to Paris. Around the turn of the century, it passed through the most prestigious collections in Europe, including the Wildensteins and Georges Hoentschel. It then traveled to the United States, where it graced the collections of Pierpont Morgan and the Knoedler Gallery, before coming to rest in 1943 among the treasures of the Frick Collection in New York, where it has watched gracefully over the Garden Court ever since.

The statue's remarkable qualities have attracted the attention of aficionados of Gothic art from around the world, and numerous facsimiles have been made in plaster or bronze to stand in places as diverse as the Sainte-Chapelle and the Musée des Monuments Français in Paris, the garden of the painter Le Sidaner in Gerberoy in Picardy, and the Pushkin Museum in Moscow. Seized with remorse, the Marquis de Talhouët-Roy commissioned a bronze copy, thus restoring the château's guardian angel to its former place.

PAGE 38
A recumbent tomb effigy discovered in the cellars of the château
and displayed in the vestibule is a reminder of the medieval origins of Le Lude.
In 1912, the architect Alcide Lafargue identified it as the fifteenth-century
effigy of Jeanne de l'Épine, mother of Jehan de Daillon.

PAGE 39
Full-length portrait of Jacqueline de La Fayette,
wife of Guy de Daillon, second Comte du Lude.

French Château Living: The Château du Lude

The Château under the de Daillon Family, from Earldom to Dukedom
1457–1685

When Jehan de Daillon (1423–1481) bought the castle, the scale of the restoration works that confronted him prompted him to turn to René, Duke of Anjou and King of Naples. Good King René, as he was known, had attracted the finest artists and craftsmen to his court, entrusting them with the task of rebuilding Anjou after the ravages of the Hundred Years' War. Jehan de Daillon was chamberlain to René's arch enemy, King Louis XI of France, but this did not prevent a friendship from developing between the new lord of Le Lude and the duke, who put de Daillon in the hands of his architect, Jean Gendrot.

The works to be undertaken at Le Lude were no longer a matter of rebuilding the damaged fortifications in their entirety, but rather of building on what remained to transform a fortress into a sumptuous Renaissance château. The scale of the project was unprecedented. Gendrot and his craftsmen set up their quarters in the town in 1479, and embarked on a major building program that in the end was to outlive them, taking two generations to complete. The memory of their presence is preserved to this day in the magnificent Maison des Architectes and rue Gendrottière in the town of Le Lude.

The defensive character of the medieval stronghold gradually disappeared, to be replaced by a profusion of Renaissance detail that reached its apogee in the years between 1510 and 1525. Jehan's son, Jacques (d.1533), fought in the military campaigns of Louis XII and François I, and in Italy he discovered the exuberance of the artistic flowering of the Renaissance, which was to have such a major influence in France. As the châteaux of Azay-le-Rideau, Chambord, and Blois were transformed into jewels of Renaissance architecture, so the lords of Le Lude made use of the skills of the many Italian craftsman who came to work in the Loire Valley.

The old castle walls, recently pierced with large windows, were adorned with pilasters, medallions, and pediments worthy of an Italian palazzo. The elegant composition known as the François I facade is considered by historians as one of the last surviving examples of Italian Renaissance architecture on a French château.

FACING PAGE
Since around 1787, a portico has linked the north and south wings
and closed the courtyard of the new château facing the wing built by the architect
Vincent Barré. General de Talhouët was the first to have the idea of
covering the courtyard, in order to give a ball there in 1840. Since then,
the *cour d'honneur* has been the setting for many festive occasions.

The Château du Lude: A Thousand Years of History

The internal decorations were similarly lavish, and the great halls—now bathed in light—were lined with frescoes, painted paneling, and brilliantly colored tapestries. These embellishments continued under Guy de Daillon (c.1530–1585), who as a boy was page to Henri de Navarre, and François (d.1619), who enjoyed the privilege of entertaining King Henri IV at Le Lude on several occasions.

The Studiolo, the most sumptuously decorated of the château's rooms, bears witness to the full magnificence of the times. The outstanding paintings that cover its walls and ceiling were executed in 1560 by artists of the school of Raphael. The ceiling paintings bear similarities to the grotesques in the Raphael rooms at the Vatican. The wall paintings, on the theme of fidelity, illustrate Noah's Ark, the story of Joseph and his brothers, Jacob at the well, and a scene inspired by the *Triumphs* of the Italian poet Petrarch. The subjects of the paintings were taken from "catalogs" that circulated among the artists of different countries at the time, hence the same Noah's Ark scene is to be found executed in marquetry in the sublime sacristy of the Certosa di San Martino in Naples.

Henri de Daillon (c.1622–1685), Grand Master of the Artillery and Lieutenant General of the Army under Louis XIV, was the last and most illustrious scion of the family. A man of great charm, with a deep interest in both the arts and literature, according to his close friend the Marquise de Sévigné, he abandoned Le Lude for the attractions of the court of the Sun King at Versailles.

In 1675, he obtained the title of *duché-prairie* for his lands at Le Lude. An inventory drawn up after his death in 1685, only discovered very recently, lists a rich collection of furnishings and artworks in the rooms at Le Lude, including a hundred or so tapestries and over three hundred paintings, as well as rich fabrics and silverware.

The de Daillons were the longest dynasty in the château's history. Their successors have perpetuated their memory, and in all the various restoration campaigns the château has undergone, their legacy has always been clearly displayed. Their monograms and arms—a silver cross on an azure ground—embellish chimney breasts, carved door panels, stained glass windows, and coffered ceilings. To this day, the de Daillon coat of arms forms part of the town crest of Le Lude.

FACING PAGE
Portrait of Henri de Daillon, Duc du Lude.
"I have conveyed to you that the grand master is Duc [du Lude];
he dare not complain. He will be a Marshall of France in the leading carriage,
and the manner in which the king [Louis XIV] has spoken far outstrips
the honor that he has received," wrote the Marquise de Sévigné–who did not
conceal her penchant for Henri de Daillon–in 1675.

French Château Living: The Château du Lude

ABOVE, FACING PAGE, AND PAGE 46

The Henri IV bedchamber has retained its magnificent seventeenth-century paneling, painted with vases of flowers and perfect for concealing hidden doors. The highly unusual chimneypiece is composed of consoles supporting slender colonettes that frame a portrait of the king.

PAGE 47

A bouquet of "Marie Pavic" roses stands beside the ivory toilet set of Marguerite, Marquise de Talhouët-Roy, on a dressing table covered with a cloth embroidered with the Bourbon royal crown.

PAGES 48–49
The initials "I.B." engraved on this elegant crystal service
are the monogram of Princess Isabelle de Bragance, daughter of Pedro II,
last Emperor of Brazil, and grandmother of the Comtesse de Nicolaÿ.

FACING PAGE AND ABOVE
The mantelpiece frieze is painted with the letter "H"
and fleur-de-lis signifying Henri's presence.

DE PVTIPHAR SA FEMO
SANS VERTV
SA CHASTETE
EPROVVE
DVRE
MENT

French Château Living: The Château du Lude

PAGES 52–53 AND ABOVE
On the wall of the Studiolo, the artist has painted copies of some
of the miniatures in the manuscript of the *Triomphes* of Petrarch, executed for
Jehan III de Daillon. He also found inspiration in Bernard Salomon's engraved
illustrations to the *Quadrins historiques de la Bible* by Claude Paradin.
Here, Rachel is guiding her father's flock.

FACING PAGE
Each of the eight faces of the ogival vault is decorated with foliage motifs,
grotesques, and little figures, in the style of the school of Raphael.

French Château Living: The Château du Lude

"[Jacques de Daillon] wanted to achieve at Le Lude what François I was doing at the Louvre, Fontainebleau, Compiègne, Chambord, and so many other places: taking the ruins of the old military fortress and erecting upon them a palace that was more in keeping with the tastes of his century and of the elegant ways that he had learned at the French court, which was so famous at this time for its luxury and splendor."

Le Monde illustré, no. 28, October 24, 1857

FACING PAGE
A bouquet of "Meg," "Cornelia," and "Felicia" roses stands in front of a portrait of Marie-Antoinette, in oil on canvas by an unknown artist.

PAGE 58
By this charter drawn up in 1715, the Duc de Roquelaure, heir to the last of the de Daillon family, invested the Seigneur des Aulnoies with the office of Capitaine des terres du Lude. A coat of arms is pinned to this manuscript.

PAGE 59
Marguerite de Béthune, second wife of Henri de Daillon, was lady-in-waiting to the Duchesse de Bourgogne, mother of the future King Louis XV.

Jouissance de La Charge de Capitaine de Ch[evau-légers]
dud[it] S[ieur] de Champchevrier

Gaston Jean Baptiste
de Biran de Puiguillen et de Lavardens
Saint Barthelemy, de Cancon, Cassenuil,
general des armées du Roy Gouverneur de
Crancin de la Succession de M. le Duc
qui nous ont esté rendus par led[it] S[ieur] Senocq
La Chesardiere, Nous ont Engagé pour marq[ue]
de la mesme son fils de la Charge de Lieut[enant]
d'autant plus recomoistre les mesures
accordons et donnons par ces presentes

The Château du Lude: A Thousand Years of History

FACING PAGE
The morning light casts a golden glow over the tuffeau stone and throws
into relief the neoclassical decorations of the facade, with its bosses, modillions,
niches, garlands, and curved window pediments.

ABOVE
The tympanum of the pediment bears the arms of the inhabitants who
commissioned the château's modern wing: a marquess's coronet unites the wolves'
heads of the de La Vieuvilles and the pinecones of the de Talhouëts.

French Château Living: The Château du Lude

Duvelaër of the East India Company and his Descendants
1750–1810

For merchants who were prepared to take risks in the eighteenth century, the East India Company could prove the route to making a fortune. Once trading posts had been established along the coasts of China, these merchant adventurers launched their cargo ships to sail the high seas. Joseph Julien Duvelaër was one of these bold traders, and he is remembered for being the first to circumnavigate the monsoon winds that had hitherto brought shipping to a halt for two months of the year by sailing via the Philippines.

The archives at Le Lude contain details of the precious cargoes of gold, porcelain, spices, and silk brocades with which he filled the holds of his ships, and which made him one of the wealthiest men in France under Louis XV. But, perhaps weary of the perils of the sea, or possibly because he sensed the imminent downfall of the East India Company, he decided to end his career in merchant shipping and return to France. It was his search for a suitable estate that brought him to Le Lude.

After two generations of neglect, the château was ripe for modernization. Duvelaër embarked on an ambitious program of works, setting out to obliterate all traces of old-fashioned military architecture from his new residence. He died before he could complete these works, and it was his niece, the Marquise de La Vieuville, née Françoise Butler, who inherited the château. It is to her that we owe most of the changes that gave the château the unique profile that we see today. The daughter of a merchant ship-owner, the marquise inherited an ambitious spirit and was not afraid of taking risks. Undaunted by the scale of the domain that she had inherited, she left her Brittany estates in the care of her husband in order to devote herself to Le Lude. There she engaged the services of one of the most brilliant architects of the age, Vincent Barré, a pupil of Gabriel, who had demonstrated his talents at the Château du Marais outside Paris and at Montgeoffroy in the Loire Valley.

At Le Lude, he achieved the tour de force of integrating a new wing in neoclassical style between two Renaissance towers and—even more remarkably—went out of his way to preserve the Renaissance decorations of the south face, as well as the marble courtyard added in the seventeenth century.

FACING PAGE
Two elegant Chinese ladies converse on board a junk, a detail
from an eighteenth-century Chinese lacquer commode.

French Château Living: The Château du Lude

ABOVE
Portrait of Joseph Julien Duvelaër, oil on canvas, by an unknown eighteenth-century artist, from the collections of the Musées de Vitré, on loan to the Musée de la Compagnie des Indes, in Port-Louis.
FACING PAGE
On the card table, a bouquet of peonies, syringa, and "Felicia" roses.
PAGE 66
Joseph Julien Duvelaër's correspondence with the trading counters in Canton is preserved in his archives, along with the cargo logs for his vessels.

The Château du Lude: A Thousand Years of History

At the same time, he planned a new tower on the western corner in order to lend symmetry to the building. This was still at the planning stage when the Revolution broke out in 1789, putting an end to work on the fabric of the building and on the interior decorations. For the Marquise de La Vieuville, there was no question of deserting her beloved Le Lude, despite the alarm and urgent pleas of her steward. His protests were in vain, however: despite much of the château's archives and furniture being seized by the Revolutionaries, the marquise's vigilant presence ensured that the château survived this turbulent period largely unscathed.

PAGE 67
Mirror painting of the wife of Joseph Julien Duvelaër, painted in France.
She wears a pendant signifying her noble birth and holds a white "China" rose.

FACING PAGE
In celebration of the two hundred and fiftieth anniversary
of the acquisition of Le Lude by Duvelaër, Thierry Bosquet, artist,
stage designer for opera and theater, and a friend of the family, designed
this costume of a Chinese princess for the mistress of the house.

ABOVE
In the grand salon, a nineteenth-century Japanese
vase with floral decoration.

French Château Living: The Château du Lude

"[T]he great achievement of [Marguerite de Talhouët-Roy] lay in taking this residence and—while on the whole respecting its existing styles and in spite of the scale and height of the rooms—endowing it with comfort, warmth, and privacy."

※

Aux jours d'autrefois, **CHRISTIAN DE NICOLAŸ**, 1980

PAGES 70–71
In the heart of the château, the oval-shaped grand salon was designed in the late eighteenth century by the architect Vincent Barré. He had the ingenious idea of creating four corner niches backed by mirrors, so creating an illusion of greater depth.

PAGE 72
In honor of the marriage of his daughter Léonie to Auguste de Talhouët-Roy in 1847, Admiral Adèle de Rigny presented Le Lude with a piano by Érard, the finest piano maker of the time.

PAGE 73
Pastel portrait of the Comte de Provence as a child, after Maurice-Quentin de La Tour. The future Louis XVIII wears the ribbon of the Ordre du Saint-Esprit.

PAGES 74–75
In the center of the grand salon, the fire has been lit for the evening.

FACING PAGE
Each of the bedrooms is decorated in a different style. In the Louis XV bedchamber, sober paneling frames an overmantel mirror highlighted in gold leaf.

French Château Living: The Château du Lude

PAGE 79
Following family tradition, on Palm Sunday branches of box from the garden are blessed at mass, and are then hung in the bedrooms, as here under the bed canopy in the Louis XV bedchamber.

PAGE 78, ABOVE, AND FACING PAGE
The armoires of the château have preserved a remarkable collection of male ceremonial attire from the late eighteenth century.

French Château Living: The Château du Lude

ABOVE AND FACING PAGE
The small Louis XVI bedchamber has a *lit à la polonaise* with hangings, and is topped
with the plumes of four carved feathers that are so characteristic of these beds.
A hidden door in the paneling.

PAGES 84–85
Snow is an unusual and magical sight at Le Lude, casting its reflections
on the glowing facade and picking out the shapes of the parterres in the Jardin
de l'Éperon, laid out on the former defensive spur.

The Château du Lude: A Thousand Years of History

FACING PAGE AND ABOVE
The Chambre de l'Altesse precedes the Studiolo. Elegant and
comfortable, it has green paneling and a *lit à la polonaise* with red hangings.
For many years, it was the bedroom of Princess d'Orléans-Bragance,
née Maria-Pia de Bourbon-Siciles, mother of de Pia de Nicolaÿ.

PAGES 88–89
Design for a tapestry, painted on cardboard, preserved at Le Lude.
On the dressing table is the princess's ivory toilet set.

French Château Living: The Château du Lude

"Going to see the linen maids … was to enter an exclusive world. … to savor the scents—damp, steamy, and strange—of freshly washed and ironed linen.… It was to admire the deft and meticulous skill they brought to their work. It was to glimpse unconsciously, through the dedication with which they carried out their tasks, the inner motivations that inspired them: devotion, pride in work well done, and a love of their métier."

Aux jours d'autrefois, **CHRISTIAN DE NICOLAŸ**, 1980

FACING PAGE
Household linen embroidered with the initials M. T. is from the trousseau of "Bonne-Maman Marguerite," the Marquise de Talhouët-Roy.
PAGE 92
The washstand in the Chambre de l'Altesse as it used to be, with its ewer, bowl, and jug decorated with the marquess's coronet. In the corner is a pair of Capodimonte porcelain cherubs.
PAGE 93
Portrait of Princess Marie-Amélie de Bragance, around 1840. The daughter of Emperor Pedro I of Brazil was the first fiancée of the future Emperor Maximilian I of Mexico.

French Château Living: The Château du Lude

"How can one begin to convey … the nature of life in a grand château fifty years ago? … During my childhood, life at Le Lude could best be compared to that of a minor court. And, moreover, Madame de Talhouët received guests there in a rather queenly fashion."

Mémoires de Blanche d'Adhémar de Lantagnac (1874–1954), written in 1934

PAGES 94–95
The morning mist lifts beneath the grand terrace,
along the lower garden.

FACING PAGE AND PAGE 98
The baldaquin of the Restoration bed in the Empire bedchamber,
with gilded decoration and Lyon silk hangings.
When Queen Elizabeth The Queen Mother visited Le Lude
in 1984, she slept in the Empire bedchamber, with its view over
the gardens and the valley of the Loir.

PAGE 99
Bowl in Paris porcelain on a biscuit porcelain stand in the form
of a seated Egyptian woman.

The Château du Lude: A Thousand Years of History

"To entertain is to serve, it has been said. If entertaining under any circumstances demands an effort, a commitment, giving of oneself, there are some occasions when it may truly become burdensome. On these occasions, our grandmother would surpass herself."

Aux jours d'autrefois, **CHRISTIAN DE NICOLAŸ**, 1980

FACING PAGE
Detail of the Empire-style *athénienne* in gilt bronze with legs embellished with dolphins.

PAGES 102–4
General Frédéric de Talhouët was deeply attached to his sister Françoise, whom the poet Alfred de Musset called his "godmother." Portrait by Robert Lefèvre. Horace Vernet, *Portrait of Général Marquis de Talhouët* [center, facing the viewer] *surrounded by his Staff*, 1818–19, private collection.

PAGES 105–7
The staircase in the south vestibule. Designed by Louis Parent around 1890, the staircase is highly unusual in rising only a single flight to the first floor.

French Château Living: The Château du Lude

ON THE FESTIVITIES HELD AT LE LUDE ON OCTOBER 7, 1857

"The festivities were worthy of this splendid residence. We shall not undertake to give a detailed description.... We shall simply offer a view of the grand salon, ... which rivals the most splendid of palaces in éclat and magnificence."

Le Monde illustré, no. 28, October 24, 1857

PAGE 108
The Green Salon is the sitting room used by the family in the summer months, under the gaze of the ladies of Le Lude. Laid out to plans by Vincent Barré in the late eighteenth century, it precedes the central Grand Salon.
PAGE 109
Portrait of the two sisters of Léonie de Talhouët-Roy, the Duchess of Padua and the Comtesse de Lagrange, by court painter Franz Xaver Winterhalter, 1841.
FACING PAGE
Gallica roses and cornflowers, a detail from the Winterhalter painting.
PAGES 112–13
Engraving from issue 28 of *Le Monde illustré*, showing the grand ball given at Le Lude by the Marquis and Marquise de Talhouët-Roy on October 7, 1857.

French Château Living: The Château du Lude

ABOVE AND FACING PAGE
The billiard room, furnished with Regency chairs covered in Beauvais tapestry.
On the right hangs a full-length portrait of Alexandrine Roy, Marquise de Talhouët,
painted by François-Joseph Kinson in 1816; on the left is a portrait
of the children of Auguste de Talhouët-Roy, by Édouard Dubufe in 1855.

PAGES 116–17
A summer bouquet of alstroemerias, stems of linden blossom,
sprays of redcurrants, nepeta, and miscanthus, and the portrait
of the Talhouët-Roy children, René and Marie-Élisabeth.

French Château Living: The Château du Lude

The Talhouët-Roy Family at Le Lude
New Vistas for the Château, 1810–1948

A ubiquitous feature of the château's interior decorations is the ermine of Anne de Bretagne, which recalls the Breton origins of the Talhouët family. Their name would be linked with Le Lude for nearly two centuries.

The battlefields of the Napoleonic Wars forged the characters and courage of many of the Grande Armée's grenadiers. Among them was Colonel Frédéric de Talhouët, who was awarded his stripes by Napoleon at the Battle of Borodino, and who, after the debacle of Waterloo, returned to his parents' estate and to Le Lude. In 1817, he married Alexandrine Roy, daughter of Comte Antoine Roy, future Minister of Finance under Louis XVIII and Charles X.

Frédéric left the army with the rank of general, to devote himself to regional politics and to the policy then in favor of dividing the country into departments. With Alexandrine, and with the support and wise advice of her father, he re-embarked on the campaign of interior decoration that had been started by the previous generation before the Revolution.

A château is nothing without its lands, however, and his lengthy visits there gave the marquis a taste for agriculture and livestock breeding, the fruits of which contributed to the income of the estate. To tackle the Malidor marshes, stretching along the banks of the Loir opposite the gardens, the marquis called in engineers to install a drainage system and transform the plain into a large area of farmland and gardens, to be planted following the principles set out by the Comte de Choulot, the famous landscape architect.

In 1836, the marquis celebrated the restored glories of Le Lude with a lavish ball, with—as the press reported at the time—fifteen hundred guests waltzing through its glittering salons and in its *cour d'honneur*, covered for the occasion.

FACING PAGE
Léonie Honnorez, shown here in a portrait by Édouard Dubufe,
was wife of Auguste, Marquis de Talhouët-Roy.
PAGES 120–21
The sun rising over the valley of the Loir. As the mist lifts from the pasture,
the great oaks are reflected in the mirror-like river.

French Château Living: The Château du Lude

It might have been imagined that this would be enough, and that work would stop there, but this would fail to take into account the enterprising spirit of Frédéric and Alexandrine's son, Auguste de Talhouët-Roy, another member of the family on whom fortune was to smile. Like his father, the young marquis decided to go into politics, and, as we have seen, he became, successively, regional councillor, parliamentary deputy, senator, and Minister of Public Works under Napoleon III. His wife, Léonie Honnorez, who came from a Belgian family of wealthy and resourceful entrepreneurs, was also to influence the marquis's plans to undertake new challenges at Le Lude.

From the middle of the nineteenth century, they embarked on a massive renovation campaign involving four architects, two renowned landscape architects, and the inestimable skills of teams of local craftsmen. Their son, René de Talhouët-Roy, and his wife, Marguerite des Monstiers Mérinville, were to see this work to completion at the outbreak of World War I. It began with the building of the north tower that had been planned before the Revolution, which became known as the Chambord tower because of its lantern copied from the royal château, and which housed the ceremonial staircase and the great library. It then continued with the roofscape, with its elegant finials and brick chimneys proudly bearing the Talhouët-Roy monogram.

The astonishing discovery of the paintings in the Studiolo in 1856 marked a turning point in the history of Le Lude. From this date, the Talhouët-Roy dynasty set out to evoke the sumptuous splendors of the Renaissance in the new decorations at Le Lude, as may be seen in the monumental stone fireplaces, coffered ceilings, painted paneling, and tapestries that we may admire today. In the enfilade of salons, a succession of portraits pays tribute to these men and women who in the nineteenth and twentieth centuries demonstrated their attachment to this unique residence, restoring it to its full and incomparable magnificence.

FACING PAGE
The billiard room is lined with paneling and has a Louis XVI-style fireplace in white marble. On the mantelpiece, a pair of gilt bronze candelabra frames an arrangement of *Allium giganteum* "Globemaster," white lilac, and syringa. In front of the fireplace sits *La Chienne Lion* ("The She-Dog-Lion"), a marble statue signed "J.-L. Chenillion du Lude Sarthe et d'Auteuil Seine," an artist who trained in the studio of David d'Angers and became a favorite at Le Lude.

French Château Living: The Château du Lude

"The splendors of the Château du Lude may perhaps be equaled only by those of Versailles. The reception room, decorated in the finest Louis XIII style, with its vaulted ceiling glittering with gold and its Beauvais tapestries framing handsome ancestral portraits, is of a sumptuousness that Louis XIV himself would have found alarming."

Le Monde illustré, no. 689, June 25, 1870

PAGES 124–25 AND FACING PAGE
The vestibule and staircase in the north wing were built in the 1850s by the architect Pierre-Félix Delarue. The ensemble underwent alterations by Louis Parent in the 1890s. He covered the floor with a sixteenth-century tiled design copied from the château of Ancy-le-Franc, which had been refurbished by his uncle Henri Parent a few years earlier.

The Château du Lude: A Thousand Years of History

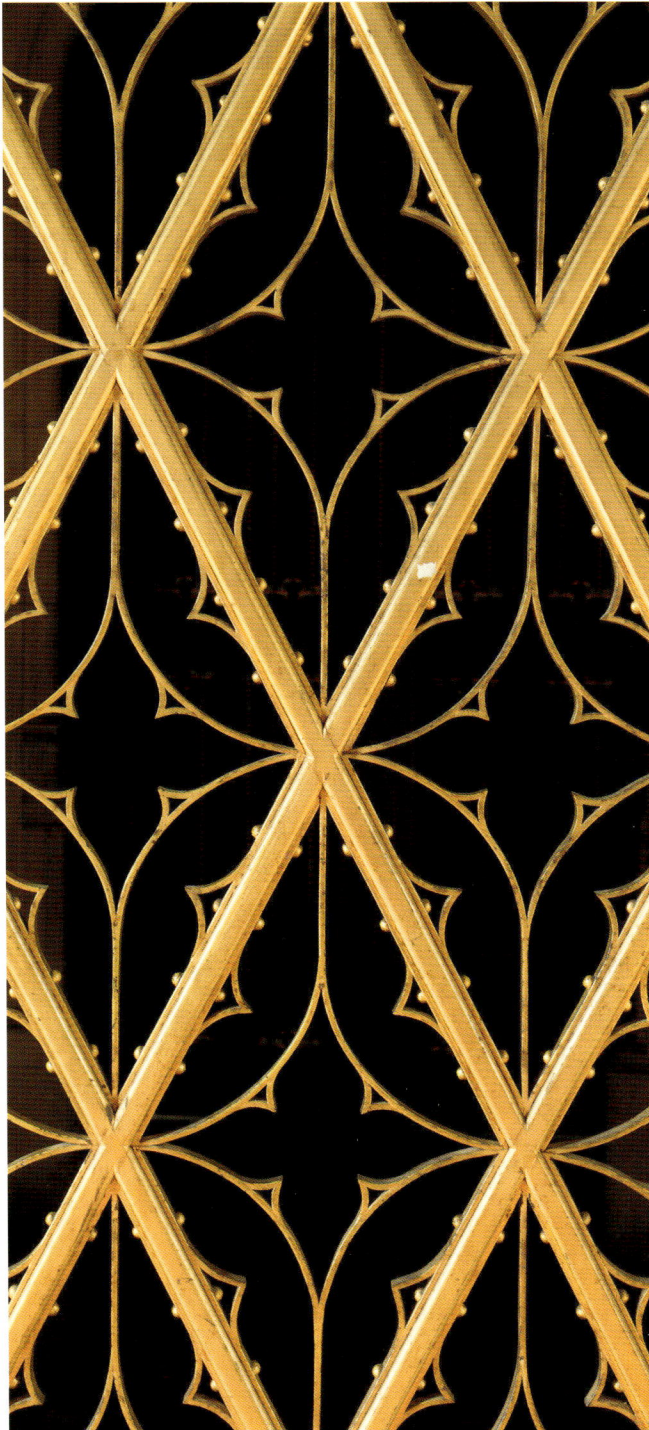

PAGES 128–29, FACING PAGE, AND ABOVE

Around 1890, the architect Louis Parent decorated the grand gallery in the neo-Renaissance style. He introduced a monumental fireplace on the outer wall. The brilliantly colored wall covering and the gilded linenfold paneling form a contrast with the natural stone of the elaborately carved fireplace.

PAGE 132

This bronze group by Comte Geoffroy de Ruillé was presented to René de Talhouët-Roy in 1910 by the members of the hunt.

The Château du Lude: A Thousand Years of History

"The Château du Lude today is what it used to be in its heyday under the de Daillon family. The Marquis de Talhouët, … the modern lord of Le Lude, has made every effort to preserve all the former splendors of his princely residence."

Le Monde illustré, no. 689, June 25, 1870

PAGE 133
The architect Louis Parent cleverly transformed a single doorway into a monumental entrance.

FACING PAGE AND PAGES 136–37
Glimpsed through the doors to the library in the northwest tower, shelves of leather-bound volumes and a bust of Comte Roy. *Fritillaria imperialis*, watercolor by Pierre-Joseph Redouté. The books are from the library of the Duc de Bouillon, and were bequeathed to the Marquise de Talhouët.

PAGES 138–39
Plan for Modification of the Terraces, drawn up in 1880 by Édouard André. Ink and wash on paper.

French Château Living: The Château du Lude

FACING PAGE
Elevation of a dormer window and chimney stacks on the north facade,
designed by Louis Parent for the Château du Lude in 1890.

LE LUDE
Détail au 1/10 des Lucarnes et
Souches de Cheminées

French Château Living: The Château du Lude

"The interior offers a succession of rooms of extreme luxury and from very different periods, from the Renaissance to Louis XVI, where one might lose oneself. There are pieces of great beauty, a bust by Slodtz, and furniture covered in tapestry in fresh colors."

Journal du duc de Trévise, 1939

FACING PAGE AND PAGES 144–45
A succession of double doors forms an enfilade in the south wing, from the dining room, through the small library and the Green Salon. The small library is also the family's winter sitting room. Portraits and photographs rub shoulders with a Gobelins tapestry depicting *Mercury and the School of Love*, after a cartoon by Simon Vouet. The *Tragédies* stamped with the arms of the Ducs de Bouillon conceal nineteenth-century literature of a more frivolous nature, such as *Vanity Fair* by Thackeray and *La Vie d'une jolie femme* by Raban.

PAGES 146–47
In the Green Salon, a pastel portrait of Yvonne de Talhouët-Roy by Frédérique Vallet-Bisson, dating from 1907. "One is lovelier, the other is prettier": so the Belle Époque paid tribute to the charms of Yvonne and her sister Anne, Comtesse de Rohan-Chabot.

PAGES 148–49
In the oval grand salon where the family entertained visitors around 1900, potted palms added a spectacular note to the decor, further amplified by the corner mirrors.

French Château Living: The Château du Lude

The Nicolaÿ Family at Le Lude
1948 TO THE PRESENT DAY

Princess Pia d'Orléans-Bragance was thirty-five when she married Comte René de Nicolaÿ in 1948. Half-Brazilian, half-Italian and born in France, she was descended from two royal houses—her father was the grandson of the Brazilian emperor Pedro II, while her mother was Princess of Bourbon Two-Sicilies—and grew up at Mandelieu near Cannes, where the Brazilian imperial family had gone into exile.

Comte René de Nicolaÿ was born at Montfort in the Sarthe, the younger son of the Marquis and Marquise de Nicolaÿ (née Yvonne de Talhouët-Roy). When he and Princess Pia married, René had just inherited the estate of Le Lude from his maternal grandfather, René de Talhouët-Roy. The couple had two children, Louis-Jean and Robert, before the young marquis succumbed to a fatal illness after only six years of marriage.

The task that faced Pia de Nicolaÿ was not an easy one. World War II had left the château in a fragile state. Would she give up and go back to the Riviera? Not a bit of it, as she related in her memoirs:

"Beloved Lude… what a comfort it was to me one evening when—at a point when the sorrows and cares seemed overwhelming—a delegation arrived from the town and asked to see me. I received them in the small salon, where they seated themselves around me. Monsieur Lelay acted as their spokesman: 'Madame, we have come to ask you not to leave Le Lude. We shall all be here for you and we shall offer you all our support.' They were as good as their word. Never again did I feel I was on my own. Quietly, a network of friendship sprang up, both in town and among our neighbors."

The first people to offer their support at Le Lude were her brothers-in-law, François and Guy de Nicolaÿ, who one after the other followed in their grandfather's footsteps in the work of the town and regional councils. In due course, their commitment was to lead Princess Pia's elder son into the world of politics, becoming first the mayor and then a senator.

The close relationship that had grown up between the château and the surrounding region was later to be illustrated in startling fashion, as Princess Pia related in her memoirs:

"René had decided, with the help of Madame Martinet [the plumber's wife], to turn the charity sale held by the little Catholic primary school into a kermesse on the château lawns. This was to be the start of a long succession of events, until one evening in 1957 when the curé of Le Lude came to see me. The theme of that year's celebrations was '*Au temps des crinolines*.' A group of ladies had gone off to Tours in secret to hire dresses from a theatrical costumier. Abbé Deniau acted as their go-between, asking if they could stage a night-time procession in order to raise funds to pay the hire charges. 'Why don't we stage a re-enactment of a nineteenth-century ball?' I asked. That was how the idea of the 'son et lumière' was born."

FACING PAGE
In 1957, the Comtesse de Nicolaÿ welcomed the first "son et lumière" show,
featuring performers drawn from the local population.

TOP, LEFT
Pia de Nicolaÿ, with her husband, the youngest son of the Marquis de Nicolaÿ,
who in 1948 inherited Le Lude from his grandfather, René de Talhouët-Roy.

TOP, RIGHT
Comtesse René de Nicolaÿ with her two sons, Louis-Jean, senator
and mayor of Le Lude, and Robert, senior advisor to the revenue court.

BOTTOM
The Comtesse de Paris and Pia de Nicolaÿ are cousins
united by bonds of deep affection.

ABOVE
Portrait in crayon of the Comtesse de Nicolaÿ by Alejo Vidal-Quadras.
The famous and talented Spanish artist attracted commissions
from the royal families of Europe in the 1960s.

TOP, LEFT
The Comtesse de Nicolaÿ's two granddaughters, Marie-Adélaïde
and Margot de Nicolaÿ, pose in pages' costumes as they wait to make
their entrance in the "son et lumière" show.

TOP, RIGHT AND BOTTOM
Memorable scenes from the "son et lumière" show recall
the heyday of the Lude: a pavane from the time of the de Daillons
and sounding the horns of the Talhouët-Roy hunt.

TOP AND BOTTOM
A minuet from the era of Louis XV
and the waltz performed on the château perron.
PAGES 156–57
Ball held by the Comtesse de Nicolaÿ in honor
of Princess Isabelle d'Orléans-Bragance.

French Château Living: The Château du Lude

She could not possibly have imagined how this spectacle would grow in size. The first of its kind, it staged the story of the château against the background of the history of France, with three hundred and fifty performers, all in costume and all from Le Lude. Michel Missoffe, a loyal friend of the family, wrote the words and lyrics, composed in verse in the style of Edmond Rostand's *Cyrano de Bergerac*; composer Antoine d'Ormesson selected the music; and François Brou, father of one of the children from the primary school of Sainte-Anne de Lude, designed the production. The set was built, and, for over forty years, fights, processions, waltzes, and ballets unfolded in the illuminated château and gardens, to the strains of a magical musical score. The success of this spectacular show brought Le Lude into the spotlight, and a steady stream of prominent figures and celebrities came to witness it and to take part, all of them received with Princess Pia's customary simplicity.

A royal visit remains engraved on local memories. Queen Elizabeth The Queen Mother was a great traveler who loved to visit France, and through a mutual friend, Prince Jean-Louis de Faucigny Lucinge, it was arranged that she should visit Le Lude in the summer of 1984. The château was thrown into a flutter of excitement. In preparation, the electrical supply was even upgraded from 110 volts to 220, in order to accommodate the royal kettle to make the indispensable royal cup of tea.

On the appointed day, Princess Pia, accompanied by her granddaughter Marie-Adélaïde, received the royal visitor and her numerous suite of close friends and staff. People still remember the exquisite elegance of her lady-in-waiting, Ruth, Lady Fermoy, grandmother of the future Princess Diana. Every evening, a footman would make the Queen Mother's favorite cocktail in the grand salon: one part gin to two parts Dubonnet, it packed a powerful punch. Every morning, the butler would argue with the château's staff over who would have the honor of taking breakfast up to the royal bedroom. The daily schedule was entrusted to the diplomat of the family, Comte Christian de Nicolaÿ, who deployed his talents to entertain the royal visitor. With the exception of the "son et lumière", what enchanted her most, it turned out, was the local market in Le Lude.

With Princess Pia, Comtesse René de Nicolaÿ, the château was therefore restored to all its former élan and warm vitality, sailing serenely into the twenty-first century—and all the more so as nine grandchildren had arrived to secure its future. Delighted to be surrounded by her grandchildren, Princess Pia has passed down to them her attachment to this remarkable château and its links with the town. The story of the new generation of the Nicolaÿ family, encouraged by the example of this woman of exceptional gifts, now waits to be written.

FACING PAGE
Queen Elizabeth The Queen Mother's visit to the Château du Lude remains etched in local memories. Here she is greeted in the town of Le Lude by the mayor, Rémy Neau.

French Château Living: The Château du Lude

"After visits in the past to Normandy, Provence, the Bordeaux region, Périgord, and Lorraine, this year The Queen Mother stayed in the Sarthe. She was the guest of Comtesse René de Nicolaÿ at the Château du Lude…. She was clearly delighted by the 'Son et Lumière' performance at Le Lude and joined in the applause."

Point de vue Images du monde, no. 1874, June 29, 1984

ABOVE AND PAGES 162–63
Pia de Nicolaÿ, The Queen Mother and Ambassador
Christian de Nicolaÿ strolling along the grand terrace.
At the entrance to the *cour d'honneur* at Le Lude,
The Queen Mother meets the château staff.

French Château Living: The Château du Lude

PAGES 164–65
The *cour d'honneur* at twilight.

ABOVE
A few decades later, it was the turn of Barbara and Louis-Jean's daughters to wed.
On this occasion, Scotland entered the family when Margot de Nicolaÿ
married Alban Mackay, photographed here with Margot's brothers Antoine
and Arnoud, and her sister Billie and brother-in-law Chuck de Liedekerke.

FACING PAGE
The marriage of Barbara and Louis-Jean de Nicolaÿ,
at the bride's family home of Hex in Belgium.

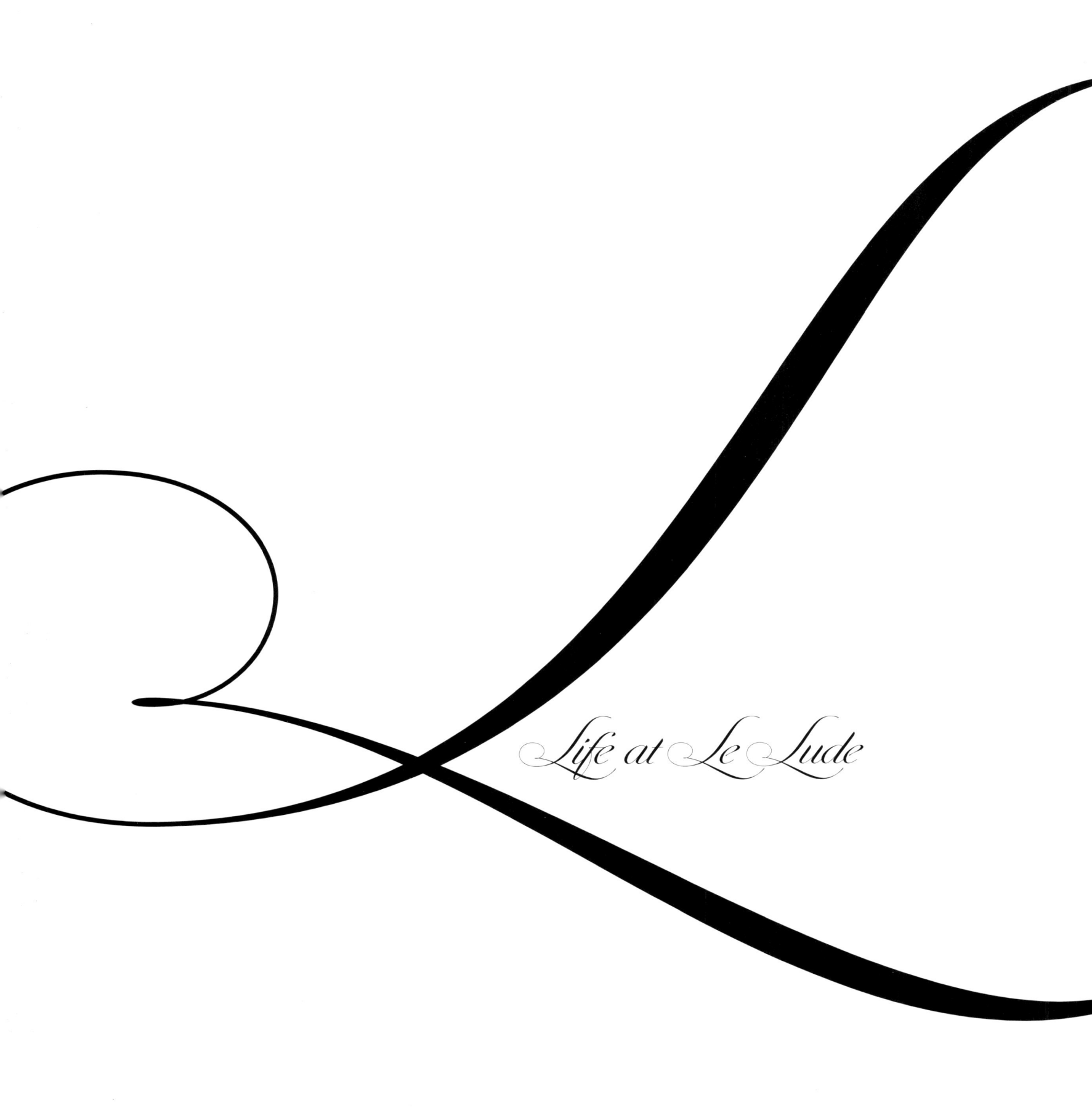
Life at Le Lude

French Château Living: The Château du Lude

Every home has its own family traditions and rituals, some of them dictated by the layout of the rooms. At Le Lude, it has always seemed strange to us that when you come into the house you have to walk through the dining room in order to reach the salons beyond. Once guests have been greeted by the dressed table, any element of drama or surprise is irrevocably lost, and some guests—as we can tell from their expressions—clearly think that after they have crossed the hall they are going straight to table, and hesitate when we invite them onward into the room beyond.

It must have been different in the nineteenth century, when the house was entered in a more logical fashion via the north wing. The room layout designed by the Talhouët-Roy grandparents created the effect they sought: the reaffirmation of the château's social function and its historical roots, and a clear desire to distinguish themselves from those substantial modern residences that, according to Villoet-le-Duc, "perished with their owners, leaving no memories behind them."

Picture visitors to Le Lude in 1865, say, stepping down from their carriage to be greeted in the entrance courtyard. They walk over the bridge to enter the vast great hall, under the enigmatic gaze of the angel of Le Lude, then they pass through the library, the Renaissance gallery, and an enfilade of four salons, before being ushered into the dining room, which lies, logically enough, directly beside the kitchens.

Before being seated at table and savoring their dinner, they can refresh their memories of French history by admiring the coffered ceiling and lantern in the style of Chambord, the Duc de Bouillon's library, the fireplaces of the same workmanship as those at Blois, the ermine of Anne of Brittany, the salamander of François I, the porcupine of Louis XII, and of course the machicolations, a reminder (if one were needed) that the fortress of Le Lude stood here before the Renaissance. Nowadays, we still eat in the dining room on a daily basis, and it is still the setting for happy family occasions, official receptions, and leisurely breakfasts, with pots of homemade jelly and copies of *Le Maine libre* and *Le Figaro* placed on the table daily, as they have been for decades.

The 24 Hours of Le Mans sports car race has catapulted the Sarthe region on to the world stage. This legendary race, which in 2023 will celebrate its centenary, mobilizes the entire region. Like other châteaux and manor houses in the area, Le Lude welcomes both racing stables and sponsors as guests. In the 1960s, Olivier Gendebien, four times winner of the endurance race, traditionally stayed with his friend Princess Pia, Comtesse de Nicolaÿ. In those days, there was nothing to stop a driver from going to wait for the sons of his hostess outside their school in Le Mans the night before the race, and driving them back to Le Lude in his elegant midnight-blue Mercedes. Two days later, Gendebien won the 24 Hours at the wheel of his Ferrari.

PAGE 168 AND FACING PAGE
On the *table à gibier*, a bouquet of choisya and "Iceberg" roses.
At Le Lude, guests' bedrooms are always decorated with flowers,
as are the reception rooms for special events.
PAGES 172–73
In the butler's pantry, the crystal service engraved with the arms
of the Bourbon-Siciles waits to be placed on the table.

Life at Le Lude

FACING PAGE
The large and sunny dining room has a highly elaborate neo-Renaissance fireplace, carved with the salamander of François I and the ermine of Queen Claude of France, daughter of Anne of Brittany. The mantelpiece bears the de Daillon arms *"d'azur à la croix engrêlée."*

ABOVE
On the cotton damask tablecloth by Pierre Frey, the porcelain service, designed by Inès de Nicolaÿ, cousin of Louis-Jean, is painted with the family crest and motto: *"Laissez dire"* ("Let them talk").

French Château Living: The Château du Lude

ABOVE AND FACING PAGE
Chocolate mousse served in little porcelain pots has been
a favorite family dessert since the time of the grandparents
whose monograms are embroidered on the napkins.
Nepeta, geraniums, choisya, and *Rosa* "Bonica" make up
this table centerpiece.

French Château Living: The Château du Lude

More recently, the Peugeot stable made its base at the château, under the exacting and paternal eye of Jean Todt, who twice led his drivers to victory.

Le Lude has also retained its royal destiny. Pia de Nicolaÿ and her first cousin, Isabelle d'Orléans, Comtesse de Paris, are very close, and share a passion for shooting. When both red-legged and gray partridge were abundant, the Comte and Comtesse de Paris came to many shoots at Le Lude, along with other frequent visitors such as President Giscard d'Estaing and the Duc de Lorge. Today, the winter is still punctuated by shoots, although pheasant and duck have now replaced the partridge, which has fallen victim to the combined effects of modern agriculture and land consolidation.

Larger gatherings take place in the Renaissance gallery, which often echoes to music and performances of various kinds. It has been the setting not only for innumerable "son et lumière" rehearsals but also for family weddings, including the recent weddings of the two daughters of the house. It has also seen kilted Scotsmen dancing reels, memorable costume balls featuring pirates, Chinese princesses, Snow White, and Peter Pan, birthday banquets—the table can seat fifty-six—and the legendary Yale Whiffenpoofs singing a cappella versions of Simon and Garfunkel hits in their customary white tie (and bringing a tear to the eye of our American guests).

When the family gets together it is usually for simpler pleasures, such as summer days on the banks of the slow-flowing Loir, with picnics and swimming at Malidor. Children and friends also gather in the kitchen garden for the great raspberry harvest, when their brimming baskets end up in the ancient kitchens and the fruit is made into jelly over the wood-fired stoves. And on Christmas Eve, hot chocolate awaits the whole family after midnight mass, to be drunk around the Neapolitan nativity scene on the marble table in the library. Meanwhile, the tall Christmas tree in the dining room twinkles with lights, guardian of the unchanging tradition that unites the current generation with all those who have gone before them in this historic home.

FACING PAGE
As the seasons change, so fruit and vegetables from the garden
come to decorate the dining room. The celadon green
of Tristar pumpkins here makes the perfect complement
to the gray marble of the Regency *table à gibier*.

PAGES 180–81
The château outbuildings viewed from the garden.
In the foreground, an old euonymus hedge has been turned
into a large maze that children love to play in.

French Château Living: The Château du Lude

"I asked her if she would like to come to Le Lude. One of her charms was that she was always prepared for anything, perhaps as a result of her former habit of spending half her time living in other people's houses.... She was ready in a moment, before I had time to fetch my overcoat, and off we went to Le Lude."

In Search of Lost Time, **MARCEL PROUST**, 1913

PAGES 184–85
Out for a ride (from left to right): the Duc de La Trémoille,
Simonne d'Uzès, the Duchesse de Luynes, the Duchesse Anne d'Uzès,
the Marquis de La Haye Jousselin, and the Marquis de Sangray.

French Château Living: The Château du Lude

ABOVE
Grooms restrain the pack before the start of the hunt.
"Until 1914, the Marquis de Talhouët-Roy possessed a delightful pack of hounds
and hunted deer with great success in the five thousand hectares of land adjoining
his fine residence at Le Lude," wrote Baron Karl Reille in 1922 in *Le Sport
universel illustré*, a weekly magazine devoted to equestrian sports.

Life at Le Lude

ABOVE
In this photograph taken in 1910, the hounds have lost the scent in the Forêt des Cartes and René de Talhouët-Roy has dismounted to give the view halloo.

PAGES 188–89
A few friends such as the Marquis de Juigné and the Comte de Clermont-Tonnerre regularly hunted with René de Talhouët-Roy, as seen in this photograph from around 1912. The ladies would come by motorcar to greet the master of the hunt.

French Château Living: The Château du Lude

ABOVE AND FACING PAGE
In the tack room are all the harnesses for the saddle horses,
marked with the Talhouët monogram. "The hunting habit is dark blue, with scarlet
waistcoat and facings, braid, white breeches and boots with cuffs for the masters,
blue breeches and hunting boots for the men," wrote Karl Reille in 1922,
in issue 990 of *Le Sport universel illustré*.

French Château Living: The Château du Lude

ABOVE AND FACING PAGE
Pheasant shooting has now taken the place
of deer hunting at Le Lude.

Life at Le Lude

"The first days of hunting, still in the grip of summer, hot and exhausting. At the end of the day, the legs suffered from having ridden over every type of terrain, stumbling over furrows, sinking into bogs, and struggling through thickets infested with brambles and across fields where maize and sunflowers make it impossible to see. A healthy fatigue all the same though, and soon obliterated by giving oneself up to sleep."

Aux jours d'autrefois, **CHRISTIAN DE NICOLAŸ**, 1980

FACING PAGE
Until the installation of the first hydraulic system in 1880, the water supply for the château stables came from the well.

Life at Le Lude

FACING PAGE AND ABOVE
The kitchens occupy the whole of the first floor of cellars under the south wing.
The gleaming copper saucepan lids, above left, are arranged in order of size.
One of the keystones of the vaulted ceiling is decorated with a carved medallion
depicting a heraldic lamb set within a laurel wreath.

PAGES 198–99
The old kitchen range was flanked by a battery of traditional cooking equipment,
much of which–including a butter churn, cake tins, cream separator,
and rows of copper and pewter pans–survives to this day.

"The service followed a classic order, with soup, fish, a variety of poultry—turkey, guinea fowl, or chicken—then roast meat and vegetables, and finally artful desserts, offering a tantalizing succession of scents and flavors to the palate."

Aux jours d'autrefois, **CHRISTIAN DE NICOLAŸ**, 1980

FACING PAGE
Great-grandfather René de Talhouët-Roy adored grapes. Right to the end of the growing season, his breakfast every day would be a freshly picked bunch of Chasselas or Muscat grapes. His gardener, Monsieur Martinet, used to relate how he would contrive to keep the vines fruiting into early November by plunging each shoot into a flask filled with water and coal, so keeping mold at bay.

Quick Redcurrant Jelly

13¼ lb./6kg redcurrants
8fl.oz./250ml water
6½ lbs./3kg superfine sugar (approx.)
Juice of a lemon

Method
1 — Place the redcurrants in a large pan with the water and heat until the redcurrants release their juice. Strain the redcurrants and reserve the juice.
2 — Measure the volume of the strained juice in fl.oz. or ml. Pour it into a copper preserving pan and add the same number of ounces/grams of sugar and the lemon juice.
3 — Place over a medium heat, stirring at regular intervals.
4 — When the mixture starts to boil, stop stirring and leave to boil for 3 minutes.
5 — Turn off the heat, skim the redcurrant mixture, and pour into jars immediately.

Pavlova

FOR THE MERINGUE
1 pinch salt
4 egg whites
1 cup/7oz./200g superfine sugar
1 tsp vanilla extract
1 tsp vinegar
1 tsp cornstarch

FOR THE FILLING
1 cup/250ml heavy or whipping cream
1 tbsp superfine sugar
1½ generous cups/10oz/300g raspberries
1 generous cup/7oz./200g strawberries
1 generous cup/7oz./200g blackcurrants

Method
MERINGUE
1 — Preheat the oven to 210°F (100°C). Grease a circular baking tin and line it with baking parchment, also greased.
2 — Add the salt to the egg whites and whisk by hand or with an electric whisk until they form stiff peaks.
3 — Gradually whisk in the sugar until the mixture is glossy.
4 — Whisk in the vanilla extract, vinegar, and cornstarch until well combined.
5 — Gently spoon the meringue mixture into the prepared tin. Cook in the bottom of the oven for an hour, until it is crisp on the outside and soft in the middle.

FILLING
1 — Whip the cream and sugar until soft peaks form.
2 — Spoon the whipped cream over the meringue and arrange the fruit on top of the cream.
3 — Keep chilled until serving.

Different fruits such as mandarins, kiwis, and bananas may be used according to the season.

Life at Le Lude

ABOVE
Once a month in the summer and fall, the old kitchens become a hive of activity as the household gathers to make jam on the wood-fired range. The red berries, freshly picked in the kitchen garden, are weighed before being decanted with their weight in sugar into the imposing copper preserving pan. The château also produces its own apple juice and honey.

PAGES 204–5
Borage flowers, echoing the blue of the East India Company porcelain, add the finishing touch to a sorbet of Williams pears with a raspberry coulis, flanked by a pavlova and a bowl of freshly picked raspberries.

Pear Sorbet with a Raspberry Coulis

This summer dessert is easy to make with an ice cream/sorbet maker.

FOR THE SORBET
4 Williams pears, very ripe
Juice of a lemon
3½ quarts/3.5 liters water
1 cup/7oz./200g superfine sugar
1 vanilla pod, or a few drops of vanilla extract

FOR THE COULIS
2 generous cups/14oz./400g raspberries, blended with ¼ cup/2oz./50g superfine sugar

TO DECORATE
Fresh borage flowers or crystallized violets (optional)

Method
1 — Peel and core the pears then chop into small pieces. Add the lemon juice to stop them turning brown.
2 — Blend the pear mixture to make a purée.
3 — In a heavy saucepan, boil the water, sugar, and vanilla together for 5 minutes to make a syrup, stirring constantly with a wooden spoon. If using a vanilla pod, leave it in the syrup to infuse as it cools.
4 — Mix the pear purée with the cooled syrup, then pour into the ice cream/sorbet maker. Leave to churn for 20 minutes to obtain a smooth sorbet.
5 — Arrange scoops of sorbet on plates or in bowls, pour over the raspberry coulis, and sprinkle with a few borage flowers or crystallized violets, if desired.

Duck with Quince and Figs

Serves 4

1 stick/3½oz./100g butter
1 clove garlic, chopped
1 onion, chopped
1 whole duck (about 2lbs./1kg)
1 jar/can quinces in syrup
12 fresh figs
Cornstarch
Salt and freshly ground black pepper

Method
1 — In a casserole, melt half the butter and fry the garlic and onion over a low heat for a couple of minutes.
2 — Add the duck to the casserole and fry over a high heat, turning it several times until lightly browned on all sides.
3 — Lower the heat and cook gently for an hour, basting regularly with spoonfuls of the quince syrup.
4 — Meanwhile, make two cuts in each fig in a cross shape, from the top to the bottom, but do not cut right through. Open them up to make star shapes.
5 — Melt the remaining butter in a frying pan. Add the figs and brown them for 10 minutes until they start to release a little juice. Remove the figs from the pan and reserve.
6 — Add the quinces and syrup to the frying pan and brown with the fig juices.
7 — Remove the duck from the casserole and reserve. Deglaze the casserole with the leftover fig juices and water, stirring in a little cornstarch to thicken the sauce, if necessary. Season with salt and freshly ground black pepper.
8 — Joint the duck and arrange it on a serving dish, surrounded by the browned figs and quinces.

RIGHT
As shooting has taken the place of deer hunting, so feathered game has made its appearance on the fall menus, alongside fruit and vegetables from the kitchen garden. The *plat du jour* is duck with figs and fingerling potatoes.

FACING PAGE
A Tristar pumpkin, Yellow Belgium tomatoes, red and white raspberries, figs, and scented geranium leaves make a striking still life on the *table à gibier*.

Life at Le Lude

FACING PAGE AND ABOVE

The great paneled linen room occupies the top of the tower. A wood stove presides over the center of the room, and propped alongside the ironing tables are trompe-l'œil Chinese vases by the artist Thierry Bosquet, waiting for the next festive event at the château.
Armoires and presses still hold the trousseaux of linen belonging to the family's great-grandmothers, as well as the stage costumes that have inspired so many "son et lumière" performances at Le Lude.

French Château Living: The Château du Lude

"A moment of cool freshness and light.
In the early morning, a filmy mist would rise over the Loir,
clinging to the river's course; the dew would linger
on the lawns; the crunch of gravel under the gardeners'
rakes would echo round the towers; and watering cans
would spray the flowers with iridescent fans of rain."

Aux jours d'autrefois, **CHRISTIAN DE NICOLAŸ**, 1980

FACING PAGE
In the middle of the kitchen garden is the gardener's cottage,
with a hipped roof above a cornice with modillions.

Life at Le Lude

FACING PAGE

You only have to plant a *pêche de vigne* pit in order to have a peach tree laden with fruit a few years later. This late variety, first cultivated by vignerons in the Lyonnais region, has red flesh that makes a delicious compôte flavored with tarragon.

ABOVE, LEFT AND RIGHT

The gardener wheels a barrow filled with the day's harvest to the kitchens. Williams pears are particularly happy in the soil at Le Lude.

French Château Living: The Château du Lude

ABOVE
Moutonne, a Soay ewe adopted by the family. The "Le Lude raspberry," has grown in the garden forever. The Savoy cabbages are one of the kitchen garden's most handsome sights.

FACING PAGE
Dahlias, cosmos, asters, and goldenrod grow in profusion.

PAGES 216–17
The Royale ordinaire or Royale hâtive cherry, known in English gardens as the Early Duke, a plate from the *Traité des arbres fruitiers* by Henri-Louis Duhamel du Monceau.
In the orchard, Napoleon bigarreaux cherries, crisp and delicious, are ready to be picked.

Royale ordinaire.

French Château Living: The Château du Lude

ABOVE AND FACING PAGE
Bergamote pears; Chinese chives; a slightly older Moutonne,
with horns; a drift of *Nigella damascena*. The orangery built of brick
has enormous arched french windows.

PAGES 220–21
Oleanders, plumbagos, lemon trees, and orchids
spend the winter in the glasshouse. The path to the kitchen garden
is lined with a double avenue of horse chestnut trees.

Life at Le Lude

PAGES 222–23
The gardener wheels a barrow laden with cauliflowers, Swiss chard, and Savoy cabbages past the orangery.

PAGES 224–25
In the old kitchens, jellies give way to soups at the end of the season, taking inspiration from whichever kitchen garden vegetables look most irresistible.

FACING PAGE, ABOVE, AND PAGES 228–29
Eitmeni, the first Porcelain Pekin bantam of the Lude, has grown into a cockerel of character. A freshly picked pumpkin is washed before being taken to the kitchens. In the large glasshouse, the leaves of a cutting of sparmannia. A bucolic scene with the château as backdrop.

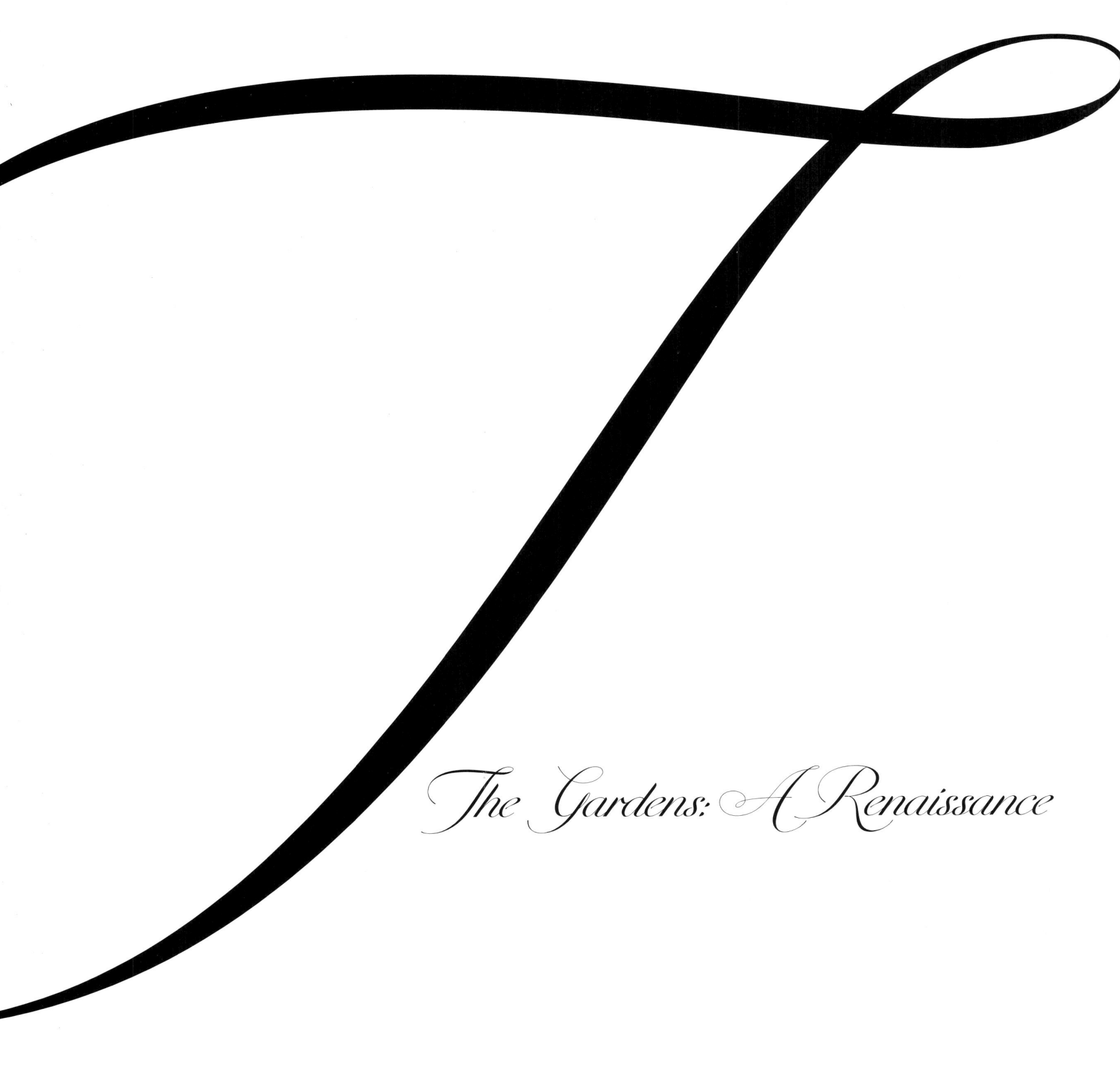

The Gardens: A Renaissance

The Gardens at Le Lude

The gardens at Le Lude owe their official designation by the French Ministry of Culture as a "*jardin remarquable*" both to their layout and garden buildings and to the setting in which they sit. The valley of the Loir and its wooded hills make a bucolic setting, and the golden light of the rising sun on the mist rising from the river transforms every morning here into a magical spectacle.

As early as the Renaissance, the land immediately around the château was arranged in terraces with sturdy foundations and edged with stone balustrades, leaving successive future generations the freedom to express their own taste according to the fashions of their era.

In the eighteenth century, the neoclassical facade was extended by the Eperon terrace, built on what had formerly been a spur (éperon) of the medieval fortifications. Throughout their history, the gardens have known many changes, with some of the most ambitious taking place from the late nineteenth century. When Edouard André presented a grand plan for the gardens to the Marquis de Talhouët-Roy in 1880, he was already a landscape architect of international renown. Trained under Napoleon III by the engineer Jean-Charles Alphand and the landscape architect Jean-Pierre Barillet-Deschamps, he could boast a portfolio of great public parks, including Les Buttes-Chaumont in Paris, Sefton Park in Liverpool, and the botanical gardens in Angers, with a sheaf of commissions that took him from England to Lithuania.

A horticulturalist above all, André was also a gifted engineer and botanist. At Le Lude, he found a site on a scale commensurate with his ambitions, where he could give rein to his full range of skills as a landscape architect. He planned a formal garden laid out along the Loir, a landscape garden for the rolling acres of parkland, a picturesque rockery for the landing stage, and a walled kitchen garden, hothouses, and an orangery to fulfill all practical needs. The entire garden would be watered by an ingenious irrigation system using the very latest techniques. By the turn of the century, a team of twenty gardeners was employed to ensure the upkeep of this impressive creation.

PAGE 230
The Jardin de l'Éperon was laid out in the late eighteenth century, when the old outbuildings and the Chapelle Saint-Aubin were demolished. As the morning light bathes the facade, the rose garden still lies in the dappled shade.

PAGES 232–33
This axonometric plan of the gardens at Le Lude was created in 2014 by the landscape architect Philippe de Kersabiec and the artist Florence d'Ersu.

FACING PAGE
"Plaisanterie" is a modern hybrid musk rose created by the Belgian rose breeder Louis Lens, from *Rosa chinensis mutabilis* and *R. moschata*.

The Gardens: A Renaissance

But the lavish lifestyle of the Belle Epoque was no longer possible or appropriate in the turbulent period that followed, with the years of Depression after the Wall Street Crash and the sufferings of two world wars. Edouard André's gardens, which had not escaped the effects of all these upheavals, were taken in hand exactly a hundred years later by the Belgian landscape architect, Augustin d'Ursel. With the respect due to his predecessor, d'Ursel revisited the gardens in order to restore their luster and carry out the brief we had given him.

The flower beds in the formal garden were removed and replaced with pools and topiary, the landing stage rockery was restored and replanted with perennial borders, and the kitchen garden was brought back into use. Only the Eperon terrace was completely transformed. Its stone buttress wall is now echoed by a wall of yews, and set between them are a star-shaped rose garden and a box maze. The rose garden is now planted with a collection of China roses, in tribute to our distant ancestor who came to Le Lude from the Orient.

In recent years, a happy encounter with the local botanist Jacky Pousse has led to the introduction of rare species from Asia and North America, which now form a botanical walk.

For over twenty years, the gardens at Le Lude have made a growing backdrop for the annual Fête des Jardiniers, at which professionals of the gardening world, collectors, and garden-lovers gather to share and enjoy every aspect of gardening. At this event, we also announce the winner of the Prix Pierre-Joseph Redouté, a prize that we have created with the Association des Jardins du Maine in honor of one of the greatest of all botanical artists, and which is awarded to the best books about gardens and botany published that year.

At the beginning of the twenty-first century, the gardens at Le Lude bear witness to changes in tastes and fashions down the centuries, while preserving the combination of grandeur and intimacy that has always been one of their distinguishing features, creating an atmosphere of gentle harmony in keeping with the spirit of this remarkable site.

FACING PAGE
Rosa chinensis "Irene Watts," one of the preponderance
of China roses in the rose collection at Le Lude.
PAGE 238
A gift of *Allium giganteum* "Globemaster" bulbs arrived at Le Lude over
ten years ago, from the Dutch horticulturalist Bert Zonneveld.
PAGE 239
Designed in 1997 by the landscape architect Augustin d'Ursel,
Barbara de Nicolaÿ's brother, the hanging Jardin de l'Éperon occupies
the site of the defensive spur (hence its name, meaning "Spur Garden")
of the medieval fortress. The rose garden and a box maze are set among
the tall yew hedges that follow the contours of the ancient walls.

French Château Living: The Château du Lude

ABOVE
The rose garden is planted with a skillful selection of drought-tolerant perennials, including Nepeta "Six Hills Giant," *Allium giganteum* "Globemaster" alliums with valerian and lavender, and *Iris germanica*.
FACING PAGE
The box maze occupies the triangular point of the old defensive spur.
PAGES 242–43
A cluster of the China roses that are favored above all others in the rose garden, framed by the golden foliage of caryopteris in the foreground and a distant view of the landscape of the Loir valley in the background. From left to right: "Clair matin," "Archiduc Joseph," and "Clementina Carbonieri."

French Château Living: The Château du Lude

"The château seemed to us to be a world apart.
You could walk for hours, or even get lost....
From the second [floor], where we lived,
there was a ravishing view over the Loir, the fields
that bordered it, and the parterres of flowers."

Mémoires de Blanche d'Adhémar de Lantagnac (1874–1954), written in 1934

FACING PAGE
Rosa "Golden Wings" opens its delicate blooms in the rose garden's white parterre.
Bred in America by Roy E. Shepherd, it is one of the loveliest of all single roses.
PAGES 246–47
The grand terrace overlooking the left bank of the Loir, beneath
the château's south facade, lends the gardens their generous sense of scale
and makes magnificent use of the topography of the site.

French Château Living: The Château du Lude

"Immense vistas opened up, the landscape of fields stretching to the horizon, dotted with movement by the horses that are bred there. I went to see the little artificial beach at Malidor, where the bluish waters of the Loir flowed past, already too cold for bathing. Then we arrived in the town, with glimpses of the magnificent towers, and behind the monumental gateway that rose in lordly fashion at the far end of the narrow streets, my gaze fell on this formidable ensemble bathed in soft light, with lovely parterres stretching as far as the eye could see."

Journal du duc de Trévise, 1939

FACING PAGE
A luxuriant planting of shrubs runs along the foot of the retaining wall of the grand terrace, scenting the air of the balustraded walk above with its perfumes.
PAGES 250–51
The superb lawns of the lower gardens unfold along the bank of the Loir, respecting the general design created by the landscape architect Édouard André.

The Prix Pierre-Joseph Redouté
A Tribute to Books about Gardens

When I was young, books, roses, Redouté—and my mother's passion for all three—were a constant presence in my life and filled my dreams. It was when I was a teenager that my parents made a discovery that was to prove a landmark in the long history of their garden at Hex in Belgium, and that would spark my mother's love of roses. A very old variety that was still growing in the garden was identified as one of the very first roses to have been imported from China in the eighteenth century. We owed this discovery to Gisèle de la Roche, the French collector of roses who was a contributor to a magnificent and recently published facsimile edition of *Les Roses* by Pierre-Joseph Redouté.

The years passed, and Le Lude became the new backdrop to my life. The new garden and rose garden we have created here are now the setting for the Fête des Jardiniers, an annual event that I have organized with my husband for nearly twenty-five years. As part of this garden festival, which has grown to become an unmissable fixture in the gardening calendar, we decided to mark the advent of the new millennium with a literary prize devoted to books on gardens and gardening. Under the aegis of the Association des Jardins du Maine, in 2000 a jury of nine prominent figures from many different areas of the gardening world met to select the year's best books on botany, gardening, and garden design. This new prize needed a name. We decided to call it the Prix Pierre-Joseph Redouté.

Our choice was prompted not only by my memories of growing up at Hex, but also by the unique place occupied in the world of gardens by the most celebrated of all botanical artists.

Born in Saint-Hubert in Belgium, Pierre-Joseph Redouté (1759–1840) was famed as the "Raphael of flowers" and painter to queens and empresses. Marie-Antoinette launched his career at Versailles as her official court artist. The Empress Joséphine raised him to the rank of "flower painter to the empress." Among his illustrious pupils were Marie-Louise, Duchess of Parma and Napoleon's second wife, Queen Hortense, the Duchess de Berry, Marie-Adélaïde d'Orléans, and Queen Amélie.

Of all Redouté's numerous works and prolific paintings, the most popular are unquestionably the albums of roses that he published from 1817 to 1824, featuring the watercolors he had painted for the Empress Joséphine in her gardens at Malmaison. Two centuries later, the Prix Pierre-Joseph Redouté recognizes the greatest talents in the gardening world today. Since the year 2000, publishers and authors, botanists and gardeners, artists and historians have gathered in the gardens of the Château du Lude to celebrate all that is most outstanding in the art of gardens and gardening.

FACING PAGE
Perennial sweet pea (*Lathyrus latifolius*) by Pierre-Joseph Redouté.
Every year, a watercolor by the celebrated botanical painter is selected as
the emblem of the new winner of the prize that bears his name.

The Gardens: A Renaissance

FACING PAGE
Held in the first weekend of June every year and famed among gardening enthusiasts, the Fête des Jardiniers attracts thousands of visitors to the château gardens, where they can browse a wide selection of open-air stalls.

ABOVE
Some nurseries have maintained a faithful presence at the Fête for over twenty years. The Guillot rose "Rhapsody in Blue" won the family's hearts and has now taken its place in the rose garden.

French Château Living: The Château du Lude

CLOCKWISE FROM TOP LEFT
Louis-Jean de Nicolaÿ; Barbara de Nicolaÿ ensures the event runs smoothly;
the interior designer Jacques Garcia and the French actress
Marie-Anne Chazel are both members of the jury.

FACING PAGE
The sweeping terrace lawn is festooned with flowers for the weekend,
displayed by exhibitors who are chosen for the variety and excellent quality of their
collections—here a glowing kaleidoscope of pelargoniums and petunias.

Bibliography

Bernot, Jacques, *Le Comte Roy, 1764–1847*, Clément Juglar, 2017

Bozo, Dominique, "Les peintures murales au château du Lude," *Gazette des Beaux-Arts*, 1965

Candé (Docteur), *Château du Lude, essai historique*, Paris, 1854

Candé (Docteur), *Millième anniversaire du château du Lude*, 1905

Murat, Inès, *Gabrielle d'Estrées*, Fayard, 1992

Nicolaÿ, Christian (de), *Aux jours d'autrefois*, 1980

Nicolaÿ, Pia (de), *Le Temps de ma mère*, Éditions JMC, 1989

Nicolaÿ-Mazery, Christiane (de), *The French Château: Life, Style, Tradition*, Thames & Hudson, 2001

Redouté, Pierre-Joseph, *Les Roses*, De Schutter, 1974–78

Thibault, Pascal, "Le Château du Lude," *Mémoire de maîtrise d'histoire de l'art. Université de Tours*, 1993

Toulier, Christine, "Le Lude en vallée du Loir," *Revue 303*, May 2015

Bulletin de la Société d'agriculture, no. 813, 2007

La Vie à la campagne, no. 50, 1908

Acknowledgments

I am grateful to Christiane de Nicolaÿ-Mazery for suggesting
the idea of creating this first, handsome book on the Château du Lude;
to France Anthonioz for reading the text with such care;
to Christine Toulier for her valuable contribution to the historical research;
to my husband Louis-Jean for his detailed information about his family
and for his advice, always sound and helpful;
and to all those both near and far who have helped me
in the preparation of this book.

PAGES 258–59
In the Jardin de la Source, early spring is a composition in every shade
and nuance of green. It is a magical moment when the delicate fronds of *Matteuccia
struthiopteris*, the ostrich fern, unfurl against a backdrop of the lobed leaves of ornamental
rhubarb (*Rheum palmatum*) and wood spurge (*Euphorbia amygdaloides*).
In the background, the leaves of the small Caroline horse chestnut, *Aesculus x neglecta*
"Erythroblastos," gradually turn from soft pink to tender green.

ABOVE
The porcupine, emblem of Louis XII, under whose reign the de Daillons
undertook the Italianate decorations of the south wing.

Photographic Credits

All photographs are by Eric Sander, with the exception of those on the following pages:

Endpapers: © Château du Lude; 16: © Château du Lude; 17: © Caroline Rose/Centre des monuments nationaux; 58: © Château du Lude; 59: © Jean-Yves Dubois; 61: © Yves Le Mao; 64: © L. Prince/Musée de Vitré; 68: © Thierry Bosquet; 84–85: © Yves Le Mao; 88: © Château du Lude; 104: © Christie's Images/Bridgeman Images; 112–13: © Bibliothèque nationale de France; 148–49: © Château du Lude; 151: © Albert Bacchino; 152 (top, left): © Château du Lude; 152 (top, right): © Albert Bacchino; 152 (bottom): © Luc Castel; 153: © By kind permission of the Fondation Alejo Vidal-Quadras; 154 (top, left): © Château du Lude; 154 (top, right): © Albert Bacchino; 154 (bottom): © Albert Bacchino; 155: © Albert Bacchino; 156–57: © Château du Lude; 159, 160: © Albert Bacchino; 161: © Château du Lude; 162–63: © Albert Bacchino; 166: © Béryl Libault; 184–89: © Château du Lude; 192, 193: © Château du Lude; 232–33: © Florence d'Ersu/Philippe de Kersabiec, 2014.

EXECUTIVE EDITOR
Suzanne Tise-Isoré

EDITORIAL ASSISTANTS
Inès Ferrand, Pauline Garrone

GRAPHIC DESIGN
Bernard Lagacé

TRANSLATED FROM THE FRENCH BY
Barbara Mellor

COPYEDITING
Helen Downey

PROOFREADING
Lindsay Porter

PRODUCTION
Angélique Florentin, Julia Mirenda

COLOR SEPARATION
Arciel, Paris

PRINTED BY
Stamperia Artistica Nazionale, Italy

Simultaneously published in French
as *L'Esprit de château, le Lude*
© Flammarion, S.A., Paris, 2017

English-language edition
© Flammarion, S.A., Paris, 2017

All rights reserved.
No part of this publication may be reproduced
in any form or by any means, electronic,
photocopy, information retrieval system,
or otherwise, without written permission from
Flammarion, S.A.
87, quai Panhard et Levassor
75647 Paris Cedex 13

editions.flammarion.com
styleetdesign-flammarion.com

17 18 19   3 2 1
ISBN: 978-2-08-020310-6
Legal Deposit: 05/2017

ENDPAPERS
Design for a tapestry, painted on cardboard,
preserved at Le Lude.